So You Want to Be A
VOICE-OVER STAR

by Sandy Thomas

In the Clubhouse Publishing
Wantagh, New York

1n the Clubhouse Publishing
PO Box 125
Wantagh, New York 11793
Phone: (516) 679-3033   Fax: (516) 679-1329
E-mail: www.sandythomas.com

ISBN 0-9672275-2-6

Library of Congress Catalog Card Number: 99-94495

Editor & Production Director: Carol A. Anderson
Cover Design: Charles J. Walsh, Chuck Starr Graphics

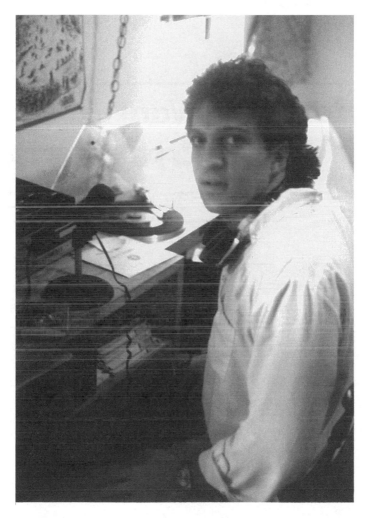

My career really took focus in my bedroom—notice the vinyl record player. I set up a make shift disc jockey booth in my room to practice being a dee-jay.

So You Want to Be A VOICE-OVER STAR

About the Author

Sandy Thomas was born in New Hyde Park on Long Island. He began his career in radio in South Florida at Hot 105 in 1986. After several years working in contemporary radio as a Production Director, Sandy was signed by one of the world's top voice-over agencies, the Cunningham, Escott, Dipene Agency in New York. He signed in December of 1992, but finally gave up his radio and free lance voice over career in South Florida, and decided to move to New York in May of 1993. He left a six figure salary with no guarantees, no income and only a dream of "making it" in big time voice-overs. A long shot for a kid who was rejected from his college radio station after being told his thick regional accent was unappealing to listeners.

Soon after arriving in New York, he quickly signed on as the national voice of the Stouffer Resort chain. He, also, voiced accounts like Maxfli, Computer City, Jeep Wrangler, Pepsi, MSNBC, Office Depot, Citizen watches, Hershey, Keebler, Pontiac, VH-1, MTV, HBO, ESPN, ESPN2, AMC, The A&E Network, The Discovery Channel, Fuji Film and Camera, Miller Beer and many other regional and national accounts. Sandy's voice is also heard as an image voice on TV and radio stations all across America. He is currently represented by The William Morris Agency in New York.

He has, truly, worked his way from the cellar to the top of this very competitive field. Presently, Sandy spends his time divided, performing national voice-work in New York City for some of the world's largest advertising agencies and Cable networks, and in his home recording studio where he provides his voice for numerous radio and TV stations across the United States. His success was not overnight. It was carefully planned. A goal that existed from the beginning of his career which began in 1984, when he was first introduced to radio at The University of Florida in Gainesville.

For anyone who has an interest in voice-overs, or is contemplating a career as a voice-over artist...well...Sandy is certainly the right tour guide!

Sandy Thomas recording at Crescent Studios in Miami.

Acknowledgments

Many thanks go out to the many people that have helped me in my career. First, I thank God. I thank my loving wife, Rebecca, for all her support, and I thank my children for their inspiration.

Also, thanks to my parents, Ed and Joan. They always supported me. To Connie Zimet for all her knowledge. Radio program director, Harry Guscott, for not hiring me at WRUF, my college radio station in Gainesville, FL—you inspired me to overcome a defeat. Thanks to Duff Lindsey, who hired me at Hot 105 in Miami in 1986—where my career really took focus. Thanks to Chuck Goldmark, Russ Oasis and Alan and Claudia Potamkin for hiring me at WXDJ in Miami as Production Director. I spent many hours in those studios practicing.

Thanks to Wayne Sandlin and Eri Salem—they had the courage to be my first and longest paid voice-over account. To Stu Dornfield, the wine cellar's on the way. Thanks to the Box Network, Tony Novia, Dean Goodman, and all of radio for their support, especially those fire breathing producers like Jeff Thomas at KIIS in LA; Mike Madrical; Eric Chase; Brian Price; Carl Harris; Robyn Stecher from Don Buchwald; AJ in Cincinnati; Zack at WPLY; Vito at Lazer; Ryan at 93X; Doug Miller at

KMXV; Jamie at WIYY; Gene at The Nerve; Andy Safnauer; Shardan and every radio image guy I ever worked with...Thanks!

Thanks to the agents at Cunningham, Escott, Dipene in New York: Angela Dipene, now retired; Donna Mancino; Diane Perez, Sharon Bierut and Ken Slevin for signing me in 1992. Thanks to WYSE Advertising for booking me with Stouffer Hotels, and thanks to Diane Perez for helping me get the account, it was a huge confidence builder—it being my first booking in New York...thanks again, Diane. I appreciate all the support you gave to my career. Thanks to the creative team at Lee Hunt in New York for allowing me to launch three networks: ESPN2, MSNBC, and the Game Show Network. Thanks to: Bob Liebert at Liebert Sound; Bruce Kaiser at Kaiser Sound; the staff at Sound Hound; Robert Martone at RMR; Full House; Reel to Reel; and other Manhattan studios like National, Super Dupe, Soundtrax, and any I may have left out.

Thanks to my agent team at William Morris, New York—Billy Serow, Mark Guss, Miranda Levenstein and Peter Hess. Thank you to Steve Miller, NBC News and MSNBC for choosing me to be the voice of MSNBC. To Chris Impomeni and to Frank Radice for your confidence and support. The production team at MSNBC: Gordon Miller, a very talented audio engineer; Eric, Gordon's audio assistant; and a team of talented producers, who are responsible for making sure the audience is aware of MSNBC...people like: Michael Weingartner; Steve Roberts and Ramona Boone. Also, thanks to Steve Herbs who hired me to be the network show voice of the NBA's "Inside Stuff," a show that airs on the NBC network. Thank you Allison Belle at HBO for hiring me for the Jerry Seinfeld job, and for bringing my voice onto HBO. And a special thank you to my agents who have gotten me through doors I could not have opened on my own.

iv

The sample commercial and promo copy reprinted in the back of this book is courtesy of HBO, KAZR Radio, the Discovery Channel, Sony Music Corp., MSNBC, KIIS Radio, Nick at Nite, The History Channel, The Learning Channel, and NASCAR.

Sandy Thomas in his studio in the summer of 1999.

Chances are if you ever called my studio, you spoke to my mother, Joan.

Dedicated to my family.

Standing outside MSNBC Studios in Secaucus, NJ in March of 1999.

Introduction

So, you want to be a voice-over star? Okay, lock yourself into a 4 by 4 padded room, and start bouncing off the walls! You just picked a field that might just put you there. Voice-overs is one of the most competitive, insecure professions on the planet. Get used to rejection, not knowing when you will work next, or if you will even work at all! The upside? Being a professional voice talent means that you hold a job where one day's work could potentially earn you your yearly salary! You work when you want, that is, when your working! You can dress in flip flops and a tee shirt, if you choose, and demand wages that easily exceed the salary of top attorneys, doctors, and executives, even CEO's. It is fun, creative, never the same, challenging, and rewarding. A dream career? Without a doubt! But remember, any job that offers this much happiness and financial reward will always require a great effort from you. However, there are men and women performing voice-overs everyday for TV and radio commercials, industrial videos, motion pictures, cartoons, computer programs, broadcast promos, CD ROMs and more.

This book covers the basic ins and outs of the voice-over business from starting out, to getting a big time voice-over agent and competing for national network commercials in New York, Los Angeles and Chicago; or staying right where you are and working in the smaller markets.

There are lessons here that you will not find taught in any drama school or broadcasting department. Hopefully, I can give you some insight by sharing with you the knowledge I have acquired by simply being there. I will take you from the beginning, when I was a graveyard disc jockey at Hot 105 in Miami, to my relocation to New York after having been signed by Cunningham, Escott, Dipene—one of the world's most noted voice-over agencies.

CONTENTS

Chapter 8

Chapter 9

1985. My first paying radio job was at WSBR, Boca Raton, Fl. My shift was 2 a.m. to 6 a.m. on Sunday night—the least listened to time slot. I would wake up my relatives and beg them to listen to me.

Chapter 1

— *What is a voice-over?*

What is a voice-over? If you go to Webster's your search will come up empty. There is no standard definition of a voice-over. By industry standards, however, a voice-over could be described as any recorded, vocal, communicated message used in cartoons, radio and TV commercials, industrial presentations, motion pictures, computer related audio, promotional announcements for radio and TV and, quite simply, is anything that has to do with vocal presentation via media.

— *Do you need a naturally deep voice?*

No! It would be nice to have vocal cords that match James Earl Jones, but the fact is, a voice like that is rare to find. Don't be alarmed, most voice talents do not sound like that. So, no, you do not need to possess a deep voice to be successful in this business. I had a career killing, regional accent when I started that still sneaks out every once in a while when I'm in session. With the right training, you have the ability to train and control your voice. You will be able to eliminate certain vocal imperfections and establish vocal control. I will talk about training next. The misconception about voice-overs is that everyone is concerned with "how do I sound?" Remember, it is the way you say it that sells your message. You can have the best vocal quality on the airwaves, but if you cannot interpret what you are recording in a voice-over session, there is a good chance you will not be asked back. The key word is: ATTITUDE! The attitude you convey is crucial to your success. You need to get comfortable with yourself! Like yourself! Because, what you are feeling inside is revealed on the microphone.

— *How do you get started?*

Working in a field where you make your own hours,

can earn a great living and love what you do has to have a downside. The downside is competition! Lots of it! There are a lot of very exceptional voice talents in the market. Be prepared to work hard and dedicate yourself. Where do you start? Good question! People enter the voice-over profession from diverse areas, actors and actresses, singers and even accountants become voice-over talent. There is no definitive answer here. Some people, like myself, come from radio. I started as a disc jockey in Miami. The transition from radio is double edged. On one hand, you gain experience because you're reading commercials all week as part of your job. On the other hand, the disadvantage is that most radio copy is amateurishly written. Most of it is unlike anything you will ever find in a real life voice-over session. Also, when you work in radio you tend to pick up many bad reading habits that have to be unlearned and learned over again correctly in order to move into a successful voice-over career. The cliché here is, "he, or she, sounds like a radio announcer." You do not want that label attached to your voice!

Perhaps you are not from a radio background, but everyone in the office says, "WOW! You have a great voice! Did you ever consider a career in voice-overs?" It happens all the time. Remember what I said. A pretty voice is only the beginning. There are things like inflection, mic presence, popping p's, romancing copy, line reading. Wait a minute, I'm moving too fast! There is a lot to this voice-over game.

So, where do you start? First, listen! Turn on the TV or the radio and listen to the commercials—the national ones. Listen for how the voice-overs sound. Record the commercials. Listen for the attitudes that are conveyed. Listen for how the message is spoken. Listen for the natural quality. Listen to all different styles of commercials. Listen, and then listen some more!

Training is crucial! To start in this business without it, puts you at a clear disadvantage. You probably won't find a solid voice-over class on any college campus, however, do not pass on any speech class. These lessons will all contribute to your skill of being a great voice talent. Your training should come from a seasoned and successful proven voice talent or casting director. Your training should come in the form of a curriculum. Some teachers teach a six week course, some eight, some ten. There is a lot to know. Always check the credentials of the teacher you are considering. A good gauge is to follow up with the teacher's former students to see if they are working. Later, I will discuss how you find a seasoned teacher with whom to train.

— *Do you need an agent?*

You haven't even booked a job and you want an agent? An agent, if a good one, will only further your effort to get work. Agents will get you into places that you might never get into otherwise and, if good, will help to further your career.

Most of the reputable agents are in New York, Los Angeles or Chicago. Agents do exist in smaller markets like Atlanta, Miami, Boston or Dallas, and some will allow you to list yourself with more than one. A good agent will gain you access to some substantial auditions. Spend some time researching the agent you are considering, and never, never pay a fee. A legitimate agent should never request any up-front money in order to sign you. They make a standard commission from the work they get you. The rate is usually 10% to 15%. Occasionally, your agent will negotiate your asking rate plus his, or her, commission.

If you begin to work outside of New York, Los Angeles or Chicago, chances are, you will more often than not act as your own agent. You will send out your demo voice tapes to advertising agencies, post production houses, independent producers, TV and radio stations and anybody else who needs to hire a voice talent. You will need to follow up, sell yourself and get the job. However, there are many voice talents that live outside of New York, Los Angeles and Chicago that have agent representation there, and compete for the big national voice-over work, too. They just choose not to live in the three major voice-over markets.

Well, now you know that you need some solid training before you can start voicing national commercials for McDonald's or Pepsi. You, also, learned that an agent is not needed when just starting out. It took me eight years until I was signed. But, hold on, there is still a lot to learn!

The cost for training, of course, varies with the teacher. An estimate would be from $600 to $1200 and up for a reputable teacher. Ouch! Hey, you've got to have training in any profession. Besides, if you make it, you can pay that off from a single day's work, and it is a tax write off!

Duff Lindsey, Program Director back in 1986 at WHQT, Hot 105, Miami, Florida. He offered me my first break—a full time on-air position.

Sandy Thomas in 1986 spinning some tunes on the air.

Chapter 2

In This Chapter:
> *— Radio, for most this is where it all begins*
> *— Should you make a demo?*
> *— Broadcasting school*
> *— Training*

— Radio, for most this is where it all begins

Most voice talent have begun as disc jockeys on radio. Hey, nice voices are wanted on the radio. As a disc jockey part of your job description includes the job of voicing radio spots or commercials. This is how disc jockeys move into a voice-over career. Do a couple of spots, get paid more in one hour than you did for a full day, and you start to say, "I like this voice-over business." But, calm down, don't start ringing up the dollar signs yet! You have to be pretty good to get an ad man or a paying client to shove a hundred and fifty bucks in your pocket in exchange for your vocal tones.

When I was in radio I would practice reading copy. I would sit in the studio for hours and hours, practicing and reading and recording myself, then playing back my voice. Listening, and listening, over and over and over again. Man, did I listen! Michael Jordan wasn't born with a basketball in his hand...or maybe he was. No, even Mike had to practice.

Do not forget to record national commercials and then try to read the copy while taping yourself. Pick commercials that best match your voice and style. For example, if you have a young sounding voice choose commercial copy that reflects that. Remember to listen to the voices on national commercials. Do not try to copy them, just listen and try to understand what makes that read special. Someone hired that voice talent. There is no doubt that working in radio gives talent an edge. At a radio station you have access to agency commercials that come to the station. Working as a disc jockey you are constantly able to listen to agency work. But remember, even if you are not a disc jockey, but simply a listener, the radio is something you can record. If you are not in radio you should record the commercials, and practice recording your own voice using the exact words from the commercial. Then, listen to your version against the original. Hear the difference? That is how far you need to progress before you can even think about making a demo tape or applying for work.

— *Should you make a demo?*

I was in radio for four years before I made my first demo. There are no rules that state when the time is right. The time is right when you have developed all the necessary skills that enable you to enter a voice-over session and successfully complete the session. This occurs when you have the ability to give the client the read he or she needs to gain client approval for the spot. A spot is an industry word for a commercial. So, unless you are emotionally prepared to walk into a studio with the confidence to read through a piece of copy with natural eloquence, and not be nervous by the silence that fills your headphones in a room that may contain some ad agency producers, a creative director, perhaps the in-house marketing executives representing the client, maybe even the client, and, of course, the engineer; and they are all collectively staring at you; then you are ready to make a demo and get it out on the market. Remember this though! You only get one chance to make an impression in this business.

— *Broadcasting school*

Okay, you are not in radio. Should you get into radio so you can get into voice-overs? Absolutely not! Get into radio because you love radio. Because you want to be on the air. Because you love music and you are not shy about being in the public eye.

To get into voice-overs you can either train with an accomplished teacher, attend a University with a strong broadcasting department or attend a broadcasting school. There is a guide that contains a list of some recommended Universities with strong broadcasting programs and broadcasting schools in the back of this book. If you are going to attend college pick a broadcasting program where a college radio station exists. This training is valuable and will make you more marketable when you graduate. If that is not possible an internship is crucial to your training.

— *Training*

Just like any other profession, training is crucial. I cannot emphasize this strongly enough. This will be the single most important thing you do. The right teacher can refine an awkward voice and mold it into a skilled, fluid, working machine. The right trainer can eliminate a regional accent. The right trainer can teach you how to read copy, how to interpret it and he, or she, will teach you the art of inflection. A good coach will eliminate bad habits that you probably do not even realize you have. It is important to get the correct training before you begin. So, where? Who? I recommend a seasoned voice talent. One who is successful or has experienced success. There are listings of teachers in *Backstage*, *Variety*, or call a local radio station and ask for the Production Director. He, or she, is the one that is responsible for the commercials on the radio station. Ask the Production Director if he or she can recommend a voice-over class or knows of someone in the market that teaches a voice-over class. I will be developing a teaching curriculum in the future. Perhaps, it will be the right teaching vehicle for you.

I received my training in Miami, Florida from a seasoned voice talent by the name of Connie Zimet. Most of the students who trained with Connie are successful working talents today. No, you do not have to kickback your teacher if you succeed.

Sandy Thomas in 1988 on the air at Hot 105 in Miami having some fun with a record promoter.

Chapter 3

In This Chapter:

— How many reads should you do?

— Character voices

— Interpreting copy, not just reading it

— Being natural sounding on mic

— Romancing copy

— How many reads should you do?

First, what is a read? A read is a style you project while reading copy. Are you reading like an announcer on Letterman or are you reading something sexy for a cologne ad? As a voice talent the more reads you are able to do the more marketable you become. Therefore, your goal is to explore as many different reads as possible without going beyond your limits. Your teacher should be the one to discover your potential.

— *Character voices*

Doing character voices also falls under reads. They will be included in your repertoire of reads if you are able to do them. Character reads might include playing a neighbor in a spot or being a cartoon character. A character read is just that, a character. You might be asked to be a stuffy sounding rich person or a sheriff. Perhaps you are in a two person spot and you are asked to voice the wife part. You can do that. I mean whether you are a women or, a...a man. I am not getting into that! What does a wife sound like? Another loaded question! You get the idea!

Character reads comprise a vast array of reads. For practice make a list of characters. For example, number one would be a boring date, number two—a hyper customer at a store, etc. With your tape recorder, practice being each character. The copy is unimportant. What is important is that you are able to act and be that character and make it credible in the voice-over or commercial. Many voice talents make their living just doing characters in TV and radio commercials.

Here is a list I want you to try:
1. A DOCTOR
2. A CARTOON CHARACTER
3. A SNOBBY WOMAN
4. A STUFFY MAN (A SNOB)

5. A POLICEMAN
6. A HUSBAND
7. A WIFE
8. A NOSY NEIGHBOR
9. A MONOTONE SLEEPY SOUNDING GUY OR GAL
10. A DRUNK
11. A GAME SHOW ANNOUNCER
12. AN EVIL SOUNDING GUY OR GAL
13. A WITCH
14. A CHILD
15. A DAD
16. A MOM
17. A STORYTELLER
18. A DOG
19. A LIZARD
20. A RABBIT

Try these characters. You'll have fun acting. Play back the reads for a friend. Ask them what they think. This will develop your acting abilities. Remember doing voice-overs is a form of acting.

— *Interpreting copy, not just reading it*

Interpreting copy, not just reading, is exactly what it says. As a hired voice talent you are not asked to just read the copy. You are paid the big bucks to bring feeling to the words. Emotion, humor, realism, romance, credibility, whatever the director wants, you better deliver. Maybe he wants you to sound monotone in your read or, maybe, it is a commercial for cologne and you need to sound elegant, and sexy. Know what you are reading. There are certain words that must be given attention. You should develop an instinct about interpreting copy. A professional voice talent is able to look at a piece of copy, get the feel of it, and after a few minutes of discussion with the producer or director, give a favorable read after several takes. Of course, you are human and you are going to stumble on certain words. You should be able to nail it by the fifth take or at least evoke a sense of optimism with your producer that you are on the right road. So, know your copy! Understand what the copywriter is trying to say. Ask questions before you read if you are unsure. Learning how to interpret copy is a skill you should strive to master. A quality voice-over teacher will cover this.

— *Being natural sounding on mic*

Natural sounding on mic is the ability to sound real or natural in whatever read you might be doing. Wow, so simple, so easy, just be myself? That's right, just be yourself. Do not try to make your voice sound deep. Deal with the voice you have been given. Remember it is not how you sound, it is how you say it that is a voice talent's best asset. Establish an attitude. Live your life. That is what you pull from. Life's experiences will shape your personality. Just remember to be real. Find the style of reads that are most natural to you. Hopefully, those reads will be what the commercial market is after.

— Romancing copy

Romancing copy is a voice talent's ability to bring a sense of romance or sexuality to what he or she is reading. I did a series of commercials for Stouffer Resorts. They were a series of national network TV spots, and all the spots needed romantic reads—breathy, soft, subtle and natural. Those commercials ran for three years. If I could not have done the read, I would not have gotten the job.

Backstage at one of many live concerts put on for Hot 105 listeners. Two singers and Sandy.

Chapter 4

In This Chapter:

— *Terminology*
— *Rejection*
— *Your chances*
— *The sweeper business*
— *Non-union*
— *Union*

— Terminology

If you are in the computer industry you know a port has nothing to do with boating, however, you do know it is a connection on the back of the computer to which you attach various external items. The voice-over industry, also, can claim its share of terminology (including slang terms). No, don't worry, no four letter words, well, maybe some. You will not find industry slang in Webster's, nor any other dictionary for that matter. Words like *spot*. If you look up *spot* you are likely to find it defined as: 1. A particular place; 2. A mark or stain. But, in the voice-over industry it is none of these. In the voice-over industry *spot* means DOG. No, just kidding, not even close. If you hear this word verbalized in a recording session do not look down at your attire, looking for a spot on your shirt. A *spot* means a commercial or promo unit. After your session, someone may say to you how many spots did you cut? Don't reply, "I didn't use scissors to cut the spot out of my shirt!" It is industry jargon. And promo, what does promo mean? Promo means a non-commercial. A promo is a promotional announcement. When you are watching TV and you see the coming attractions to a show that is coming up next. For example: let us say you are watching NBC, you hear the announcer say "Tonight on NBC, it's the funniest new show on network television...." While you hear the voice-over, you see the action on your TV. Then, the announcer will close with "Tonight on NBC." That is called a *promo*. It is not a commercial. It had no commercial merit. It was solely aired to promote programming.

Voice-over talent get paid different rates for commercials and promos with commercials being more lucrative. Although, there is excellent money in promo work because there is a high volume of work. Once a network, TV, radio station or show producer uses your voice they will most likely continue to use your voice. It is their objective to build a familiar sound and, hopefully, your voice will be incorporated into the sound. There are voice guys and gals who do mostly promo work for networks, like NBC, ABC, CBS, HBO, SHOWTIME, ESPN, etc. They make well into the six digits, some in the seven. But anyway, back to terminology. If you turn to the back of the book you will find a glossary. If you come across a word in the book that makes you go...hmmmm?...check out the glossary.

— Rejection

Rejection is a part of the voice-over business, just like dealing with numbers is a part of an accountant's job. If you want to be a part of the voice-over industry, learn to deal with rejection! Hey, any field that allows you to make a lot of money, work pretty much when you feel like it and is lots of fun, is going to attract a lot of people. Bottom line...*a lot of people want to do voice-overs!* The competitive arena is PACKED! The odds that you will make it are not great! Wait! Wait! Relax! I did not say you cannot succeed! Besides, there are many levels of success in the voice-over business. But, if you cannot deal with rejection put this book down NOW! Be an accountant, work at the post office, be a lawyer...no, on second thought, do not become an attorney, that's worse. Seriously though, build an immunity to rejection now! Remember the old Superman shows when Superman was standing there and bullets would ricochet off his chest? If you plan on being a voice talent, you should be able to fend off rejection the way Superman repelled those bullets. Remember your voice is nothing more than a tool in a process. Do not start letting it get personal. It is all objective, some people will love your voice, some will dislike it. You will send your demo tape out and never hear from anyone; and then, the phone rings and you will answer, "Who is this" and they will respond, "you sent us a tape seven months ago and we just got around to listening to it."

Back to rejection. The chances of being successful or making a living performing voice-overs in the top three major markets, New York, Chicago and Los Angeles can be compared to professional sports. You could compare it to almost the same chances of an athlete making it to the majors. The odds are against you, however, making it in smaller markets is easier and less congested, and still lucrative. I began in radio in December of 1984, continued in radio and voice-overs in Miami from 1986 and then moved to New York to pursue voice-overs full time in May of 1993. From the beginning it took me nine years until I was ready. Everyone is different. When you are in a place like New York, you are competing against the top talent in the world and not just against voice talent, you are also up against celebrity voice talent like Alec Baldwin, Rob Morrow and hundreds of other accomplished actors. Everyone you audition against is a home run hitter. Wow, intimidating, you say? Not for one minute! Arrogant? Not at all! YOU cannot waste time thinking about that. You have to believe you are the only one for the job. Go in, read your audition, leave and never wonder if you are going to get that job. Do not worry who was reading before or after you. Did they like you? Maybe, maybe not! Just head off to the next audition! Never look back! This is a business where you will fall more than you will win. But, when you win, the payoff can be big.

In major markets, like New York, the odds are against you. Some of the biggest and best voice talent live or work out of New York, Los Angeles and Chicago. Most of the biggest advertising agencies, broadcasting companies and show producers in the world make their home offices in New York, Los Angeles and Chicago, and those companies usually cast their voice talent from these three major markets. If you want to compete in big time voice-overs, play ball in the majors! You need to establish your connections there. I will speak further about going to the majors later.

Rejection is a lonely, emotional state of mind that most voice talent live with from time to time. What do you do? Nothing! Live with it! Build a tolerance for it. Rejection will follow you whether you are a voice talent in Toledo, Miami, Dallas or New York. You send a tape out, and you never hear back. You audition, and you do not get the job. You follow up and a producer tells you "sorry, we were looking for an older sounding voice." AHHHHH! Rejection! Learn to get used to it, or choose another profession!

— *Your chances*

I already shared with you the dismal statistics of making it in the major markets. Sorry, although places like Miami, Dallas, Boston and Philadelphia are less congested and a little easier in which to find work than the three major union cities, like New York, Los Angeles and Chicago, those places, too, are filled with talented voice people free-lancing and competing daily for jobs. The difference in those markets is that most talent represent themselves. In the three major markets you need an agent and 99.9% of the jobs are won by way of an audition that is sought for you by your agent. No agent there and your ability to get work almost disappears! In the smaller markets you can contact the advertising agency producers, forward your tape and be booked from that tape without the need of an agent's representation. You can be without an agent. However, agents and the audition process is prevalent in the medium and large market cities. How do you increase your chances for success? Be good at what you do! Get the right training, practice, and then, practice some more. And, listen to and practice national commercials as I told you before in the beginning of the book. Listen and practice.

— The sweeper business

For instance, the medical field has specialized areas. There are Cardiologists, Podiatrists and Orthopedists. Each doctor specializes in a different area of expertise. The voice-over field, too, has different specialized areas. There are guys who do cartoon characters, promo reads, industrial presentations, movie trailers, commercials, sweepers and promos for radio. All of these are specialized. They all require different approaches in the way you read. It depends on what the product is. It depends on the copy, and who is hearing the message. There are so many parameters. The more areas in which you specialize, the more marketable you will be. The sweeper business is a specialized area that concentrates on radio promotional work. A sweeper is defined as a short, transitional, promotional, positioning statement run in between songs, or in and out of commercial sets that range from three to eight seconds long, and usually are not more than twelve or fifteen seconds long. They are produced in either of two formats: a voice-over, or a jingle, or a combination of both. You acquire this work by contracting with a radio station for a length of time for an agreed amount of money in return for your voice. Obviously, if you are not in the same city as the radio station you are contracted with, you would need studio facilities to record. Some guys have their own in house studio, like myself, or they use an independent studio. This will cost money which will be passed along in the total cost. Radio imaging is consistent work. Mailing lists of radio stations are available. Just start sending your demos to radio station Program Directors. I have been voicing radio stations since 1986. Since I have been in radio, I have had experience in this specialized area from the beginning of my career. My first station was WZEW in Mobile. Since then I have voiced stations like WLUP in Chicago, KIIS-FM in Los Angeles and WDVE in Pittsburgh. There is a certain delivery when you are performing sweeper and promo work for radio stations. It depends on the format in which you are performing. Nothing is the same. And the style of the announcer is forever changing. Back in the 80's, Rock and Top 40 radio used big sounding voice guys. Now, it seems, that the 90's, going into 2000, calls for a very real sounding, hip voice, however the deep guy is always needed and there is room for all types, including a great need for female voice talents.

The station voice becomes the image of that radio station. My advice is to listen to different stations. Listen for the image voice—not the live disc jockey—but listen to the voice that is prerecorded. The station voice fits the personality of the radio station. If it is a classical station chances are the voice will sound rich and articulate. If it is a rock station the voice will display a hip, cool attitude. You understand. The sweeper business is filled with a lot of talented voice talent. The field is very crowded, so you need to be on your game to compete in this marketplace.

What if you have a radio station interested in using your golden pipes, what do you charge? That depends on your arrangement. Some guys go by a set rate, by the line or promo. You can offer a twelve month minimum contract or offer a set monthly amount of voice work. When the amount of work exceeds the agreed amount, you should assess another fee for the exceeded work. Basically, you make your own deal. Your talents, and the demand for your talents, will determine your wages. A basic guideline: never allow anyone to continue using your voice without compensating you.

You can begin learning about radio by subscribing to *Radio & Records*, the radio industry's trade paper. Also, subscribe to *Radio & Production*. Contact information is listed in the back of the book. One thing to remember, radio pays the least in the voice-over business. You can make more in one day doing a commercial session than you might make in one year of performing your voice-over services for a particular radio station. However, it is still good money. And, the hours? For the most part, you are the architect of your work schedule. However, be flexible with the producers with whom you work.

— *Non-union*

When you have cut your first demo tape, you will most likely be non-union status. There are two unions with whom voice talent affiliate. There is AFTRA, which stands for American Federation of Television and Radio Artists, and SAG, which stands for Screen Actors Guild. In the next chapter I will discuss unions. For now, you are non-union. What does this mean for you? Clients love you! They are now free to abuse your talent and services. No residuals to pay, unlimited use of your voice for a one time fee to run whenever and wherever they please, and you receive no pension, welfare or health benefits. Wow! Okay, relax it is not that bad. All voice-over talent begin as non-union talent. Hey, you have to be at the top of your game for a client to deal with you as a union member. So, for now you are non-union. Your tape will say "NON-UNION" and you are only allowed to perform non-union work. There are some networks and most radio stations that do not fall under union jurisdiction. In these situations a union talent is not free to pursue this work, however, you are non-union and can.

Most major and medium markets, anything outside of New York, Chicago and Los Angeles, consist of a fairly talented pool of non-union voice talent. There you will find advertising agencies that will work with you if you are non-union. If you are in New York, Chicago or Los Angeles or plan on going there, you need to be in AFTRA and SAG, but more on unions later. What do I charge as a non-union voice-over talent? Whatever you want. Non-union means no rules, make your own deal. There are no wage limits, but as a fair gauge for a local radio spot running in a local market, I would charge $150, and for TV, I would charge from $250-$350. If you want, you could include a residual rate and have your client sign some form, or mild contract, that would bind him to your verbal agreement. People have a way of forgetting when they are asked to fetch their checkbook. Draw up a contract or get it up front. You will need to print invoices, because most clients pay in thirty to sixty days. Anything longer is extreme and at that point you will need to call Vinny and Anthony. So, work with reputable people.

Back to residuals. Let us say an advertiser makes a request for your services. Let us say it is "Tom's Used Cars." They want your voice for a TV spot. You say, "$300!", "No!" Tom says: "Too high!" You have the option of coming down. You agree on $150. Your next question should be, "How long are you going to run it and where?" Tom might say: "Wherever I want, and as long as I want." He has the right, after all, you are non-union, and he is paying you the agreed wage. At this point you might tell him that your deal is good for so many weeks of usage. Let's say 13 weeks. That means from the time you complete the voice-over session the advertiser has 13 weeks to use your voice. At the end of the 13th week you have the right to invoice again for the agreed on fee, in this case, we said $150. Some clients might go for it, some will not. If they say no, perhaps the thing to do is to charge a higher up front rate to compensate for the usage. The bottom line, here, is in the non-union world of voice-overs you make your own deal.

Let me explain about the concept of usage. Usage is where the commercial is running. You should earn more dollars from a national commercial as opposed to a local commercial. When you are union there are set rates in place, so the voice talent doesn't need to worry about coming up with a charge. But, you are non-union, what do you charge? Use this as a reference: For a local radio voice-over, charge $150. For a local TV voice-over, charge $300. Add $5.00 for each additional market in which your commercial is running. After 13 weeks bill the client again. Remember, some clients will not go for the re-bill thing. You might have to hold your breath for awhile. For a national TV spot, that is, if it runs on the Networks, I would charge no less than one thousand dollars. Remember, there are millions of viewers. You should be compensated for that reach. For a national radio spot, a radio network like CBS, I would charge $400 to $500. Use these references, but do not make them your law. Some beginning non union voice talent settle for $75 for a TV spot.

Oh, one more thing: tags. A tag is what you hear at the end of a spot. It is usually an address, or words, that make up the last line of a spot. For example "Tom's Used Cars saves you more." You might be asked to read multiple tags. Your rate for these short, no more than two line, phrases should be $50.

It is rare for anyone to begin with union status as a

voice talent. So, start with non-union. You will still be able to command a decent wage. If it takes you fifteen minutes to complete a TV spot and you have been compensated $75—that is not bad. As you progress you will be able to command more for your talents, and once you become a union talent, you will have health insurance and pension added to your compensation package.

— Union

We spoke briefly about unions in the non-union section. I told you the two unions that affect voice-over talent. They are SAG and AFTRA. The Screen Actors Guild was formed in 1933. The union that began in a one room office in Hollywood over 60 years ago, now resides in Museum Square. It has nearly 200 employees, has 20 distinctive branches around the country that serve its members, and is about 47,000 members strong. I have listed SAG information at the back of the book. Call one of the SAG offices. Find out about how to join.

AFTRA is another independent union that a voice-over artist must join when deciding to be union status. Like SAG, AFTRA also requires yearly dues. Like SAG, AFTRA offices exist in cities across the country. A list is at the back of the book. Call an AFTRA office, inquire about joining. You should consider joining both unions. The yearly union dues are costly, but they are worth it. Remember, once you become a union talent you surrender your rights to perform non-union work. You are now only allowed to work for union signatories, agencies or producers. Inquire about these union requirements when you call the SAG and AFTRA offices.

The benefits of joining SAG and AFTRA are many. Guaranteed residuals, pension, welfare and health benefits once you exceed your earning requirements, and the strength of a national union to ensure that you are compensated for contracted binding voice-over work. It is definitely the only way to go if you want be at the top of the voice-over industry. Call the union offices and inquire about joining.

You do not, however, join SAG or AFTRA until you have perfected your craft. Basically, when a union producer is willing to give you a one time only union shot you are free to join. Just be warned that once you join, you must terminate all your non-union commercial contacts. You are a union talent now, you crossed the line to become a union voice talent. Now all you have to do is get some work. Hang on! The ride has just begun.

1986. Onstage with fellow disc jockey Ricky Ricardo on Sandy's right. No, he wasn't married to Lucy.

Chapter 5

— *Finding your money read*

This is your jackpot read. The one you are hired to perform the most. Most guys and gals who perform voice-overs on a national level usually have a money read. James Earl Jones is hired to do one thing. IMITATE God. There are famous voice talents who are consistently called on for their distinct sound—their money read. People like Hal Douglas, Mason Adams, Jim Fagen, Les Marshak,

Polly Adams, Alan Bleviss, Michael Carroll, Ed Grover, Fran Brill, Lynne MacLaren, Connie Zimet and Don Lon Fontaine. These, and hundreds of other voice talents, have that money read. You just know when Donald Sutherland's voice comes through your TV speakers, or the voice of the late Fred Gwynn who made the word Maytag a household name.

How do you realize your money read? It is a read that is naturally part of your personality. It might be your natural voice, it might be slightly affected. Hey, it could be animated, maybe a cartoon character you create. It is the kind of read that you are hired for most often. Maybe you have more than one, maybe three. The characteristic of the money read is that it is unique, real sounding, commanding, credible, likeable—a read that stands out from the others. If you ever make an attempt to imitate national voice talent John Bartholomew Tucker, your efforts will come up short. His style is just so different and unable to imitate. He has a voice that people will pay for. You have heard him on national commercials for years. How about Joe Kelly, the late Ernie Anderson, Alex Rhodie, Jack Lemmon or Polly Adams? They all have their own styles. Ernie passed on several years ago. He was the voice of ABC for years—the deep voice you used to hear saying..."Tonight, on the Love Boat."

Develop your own style. Find your own read. Mine seems

to be my natural voice. I deliver this quality with a natural, easy, conversational style that seems to work. I have performed this style for clients like VH-1, Fuji Film, HBO, Hershey, MSNBC and others. Your money read might take time to develop. It might be there now. See what kind of read fits your voice the best. The right teacher will be able to help you realize your potential, and set you on the right path to developing that read. And, once you put it to work for you, you will see demand for your voice.

— Making a Demo

Once your teacher gives you the okay, then go ahead and produce your demo. Most teachers include a finished produced demo as part of their curriculum. The demo should include various reads, and it should run from two and a half minutes to three minutes, no longer. Include two sides. One side is straight reads, the other is character reads. Your teacher will help develop your tape. There is a list of publications that have a classified section including teachers and engineers that provide voice-over classes and voice-over demo tapes. *Backstage* is a trade paper to get. Keep in mind that your demo tape should not exceed your voice-over abilities. Whatever reads you decide to put on your cassette, you had better be able to perform eloquently at a voice-over session. Your tape should flow containing several reads edited together. Your strongest work should be included first. Edit each read after a 10 or 15 second duration. Make sure there are various styles of reads. Include an up tempo retail read, a soft romantic read, maybe a conversational guy up the block read, etc. Consult with your teacher about the kinds of reads to include on your demo tape.

If you are performing promo work for TV or radio you should have a separate demo tape exclusively for that. These demos should contain samples of work from stations you are working with. If you are just starting out, cut demonstration promos and sweepers. These TV and radio demos will be sent directly to the TV and radio stations. After you have completed your master demo tape or tapes you will need to duplicate them. Your teacher is not going to duplicate 150 copies of your demo tape. Unfortunately, your course will not include that service. He or she will be able to refer you to a duplication house. Obviously, there is a charge for this service. The charge depends on how many copies you request. 150 is a good number to begin with. The cost varies, you may want to shop around and compare prices.

— *Getting work*

Getting work! Only if it were that easy! You have your

demos! Your confidence is high! You are ready to enter your first voice-over session! Are you? Picture this. I will give you a typical walk-through from a national session I did for Fuji Film and Camera through Angotti, Thomas, Hedge in New York. I arrived at the studio, Photomag, in Manhattan, at 222 East 44th Street, at 10 a.m. I arrived at the front desk about 9:50 a.m. I was asked by the secretary, "Can I help you?" Remember, you are a voice, nobody recognizes you. I replied, "Yes, Sandy Thomas for a voice-over for Fuji." She says, "Down the hall, Studio C." The adrenaline begins to pump. In minutes you know you will be thrust in the middle of a national voice-over session. You are aware that millions of dollars have been invested into a campaign you are about to anchor. I mean millions! The commercials, two in my session, cost around $150,000 each to produce. Add to this the millions that are spent on media to air these messages, and you realize you are part of an important process. I entered Studio C and was met by some unfamiliar faces, and a state of the art digital studio that resembled something that looked like a NASA control room. I introduced myself to the advertising agency producers and studio engineer, engaged in some subtle conversation, and then, I was handed a script. I looked at it, conversed about what they were looking for, and then, I was sent on my way into the sound room, on my own, to put the finishing touches on what has now become over a million dollar investment. The studio engineer echoed in my headphones and asked for me to read so that he could get a correct recording level.

I settled down and gave the engineer a mic check. My engineer replied, "great, okay rollin' on one. This is one." There was an eerie silence in my headphones. It was my turn. Everything I worked for raced through my mind, I was at the top, you cannot get any higher. You know when you breath your first words of the script those agency producers will be hanging on your every syllable. They are prepared to invest heavily in your talents, expecting you to deliver a perfect, flawless read. You are aware that if you fail you won't be asked back, and word does travel. Advertising is a small business and everyone knows the same people. The pressure was on, big time! I have been here before. I paused, then I said, "It's not about saying 'cheese' anymore. It's not about posing on the couch in your Sunday clothes. It's what doesn't go according to plan that makes the best pictures. Try Fujicolor Quicksnap Plus One-Time Use Cameras with Brilliant pictures from technically advanced Fujicolor Super G Plus Film. Because life won't stand still while you go home and get your camera." Silence, then I heard a reply from one of the producers, "Great nice read. Can we try it again?" I read it again and after about five takes it was done.

As I exited the sound booth I met with the agency producers. I heard a playback. It flowed, sounded real, contained emotions. A credible read. I signed the contract, we shared a laugh, shook hands and the session concluded. A few weeks later while watching The U.S. Open on CBS I heard my voice echoing from the TV as I sat crunched in my couch. There I was, my voice beaming across the nation on network television. Are you composed and ready to enter your first voice-over session? Then, start sending out copies of your demo tape!

— *Auditioning*

Auditioning! Some talent love it. Some dread it. You need to love it! It is the only way you are going to get a job, at least, if you are in the three major union markets, New York, Los Angeles and Chicago! The misconception is that if I send my demo tape to that Park Avenue agency, they will listen, love my voice, call to book me and I will be in residual heaven. It just does not work that way in most major markets! In New York it is rare for producers to book you off your tape. Everybody wants to hear you. There are people at all levels to approve things. Your voice needs to be heard reading the script. How does he or she sound doing our product? Maybe they are going to test your voice to see how people respond to it. At this level every aspect of the creative process is scrutinized, including your voice-over. In other markets it is possible to sidestep the audition process. In markets like Boston, Miami, Dallas, Philadelphia and smaller markets, it is possible to send your demo tape to local ad agencies, and even directly to clients to get work. In New York, Los Angeles and Chicago, you usually have to audition until you build a reputation, and the people responsible for booking talent get to know your work and are confident in your talents. And still you will have to audition. Even the big name veterans audition.

Auditioning, in itself, is an art form you need to master. Be friendly with the casting directors, but do not talk too much! They have many other voice talents to hear after you. Your main objective at an audition is to put your voice down on tape for a producer or client to hear. You might have an opportunity to put more than one read down on tape. You might be asked for only one read. It will usually be you and the casting director, however, sometimes the client, or producer, or both, might be present at an audition to hear the voice talent. This is your chance to get a voice-over job. The audition is where it all begins. Do not worry about running the equipment, the casting director does that. You just get comfortable with the script, listen for the casting director's direction and read when you are given the cue.

Do not underestimate the power of an audition. Although, at times you might tire of this process. You will see a line of talent reading for the same thing. You see people and say: "Oh no, he's reading for this too? This guy is the best! I'll never get this account." Cast those negative thoughts from your head! You never know what a producer or client is looking for. You could be what they are looking for, so, get to that audition, sign your name on the sign-in sheet, wait for your name to be called and give a great performance.

— *Keeping the humor*

Do not panic it is only a career...yeah, right! I know it is not easy. This is a business that forever feeds off an appetite of change. Everybody is constantly looking for the next voice. Who's sound is in? Who's over used? No, not him, he sounds too old...not her, too perky sounding. It is out of your control. Do not let every valley get to you. Because you will hit some low points. You will hear it: "You're not right" "Your sound is too young" "...too old" "...too announcery" "Your accent is too heavy" "We are releasing you, we're going with someone else" AGHHHHHHHHHHHHH!!! Yeah! I know it is enough to drive you crazy! Find humor, in everything. You're going to lose jobs, be rejected, told you're not right. This is a business of illusions. Nothing is real, except an opinion and everyone has one. That producer thinks you are a star, the other thinks you have no talent. Forget it! On to the next audition. Remember, you are forever applying for a job. Always sending out another demo, always re-inventing your style, working on your reads, listening to what is in and what is out. There is always the hope that the next producer, casting director, or client will love your voice. And, try to maintain a sense of humor. Tomorrow always presents a new opportunity.

— Getting an agent

If you reside in a market outside New York, Los Angeles or Chicago it is not necessary to have an exclusive agent to get work; however, even if you do not plan on moving to New York, Los Angeles or Chicago, retaining an agent there to represent you will provide you with opportunities you might not be able to get on your own. So, how do you start? You start by getting a copy of *The Ross Report*. In it you will find a list of the reputable talent agents in the country. Top agents for voice-overs are William Morris; Don Buchwald; Cunningham, Escott, Dipene; SEM & N; ICM; and, Paradigm. There are others. Get *The Ross Report*. Next, call the agent you are interested in having represent you. Ask for the name of the person to whom you should direct your voice-over demo reel to be considered for agency representation. Send your reel, and hope there is enough magic on it to get the agency to want to sign you. People think you need a connection for an agent to sign you. That is a myth. I sent my demo to three agents back in 1992. One of those agents was Cunningham, Escott, Dipene. They are probably one of the most recognized voice-over agents in the world. They represent some of the most famous and most used voices like Hal Douglas, Sam Roberts, Paul Christie, and Tony Hoylen. They responded to my tape by calling me in South Florida where I was living at the time. I flew up, met with their voice-over agent's team and signed a contract. They were instrumental in kick-starting my career in New York. After five years in New York, I was represented by ICM, and then, moved to William Morris. All three are dynamic agents, and are very entrenched in the voice-over market. All of them get results. So, getting an agent is like getting another booking. You send your tape to them, and hope your style and voice is something they need or are lacking in their roster of voices. Remember, agents do not like to have too many of the same sounding voices because they are responsible for getting you work. They will not overstock themselves or some of their talent will lack work and eventually defect to other agencies.

We used to pack the house with our live outdoor concerts. A Hot 105 live concert on Biscayne Bay in 1986.

Chapter 6

— The script

The script. There it is. It might be a three-second tag. It could be thirty seconds, or sixty. Scripts come in various time frames. They all require different approaches. I have had the opportunity and good fortune to voice some big accounts. They vary from promos for local radio to promos for national TV and cable networks like MSNBC, NBC, ESPN, HBO, The

WB Network and others. You will be given many types of scripts first at auditions and then at bookings. You have moments to get acquainted with the copy, then it is on mic and you are expected to deliver. And, it needs to be flawless! Perfection! That is why the preparation and experience you get before you enter this critical process is so important! Do not underestimate training, speech classes, taking classes with a skilled voice talent, casting director, or any qualified teacher. There is not a lot of preparation time in the voice-over industry. You cannot take the script home to look it over. Chances are you will not have the option to see it in advance, however, sometimes you will. It just depends on the situation, and all the situations are different. Look at the scripts! Be ready to go, and be ready to deliver a read that is special. Believe in yourself and never doubt your talents. Your confidence is crucial to your success.

— *Adapt to your voice-over environment*

What does that mean? It means that you need to understand what you are reading and know how to read it. Each script you are presented demands an attitude, a style of reading. You might be asked to read, "This has been a presentation of NBC News, the biggest news organization in the world." You have to say that with dominant credibility. Your voice must have a serious tone...you are speaking on behalf of one of the biggest broadcasting networks in the world.

Look at the script and evaluate your voice-over environment, then get into a character that is parallel to what you are reading. You do not want to sound unsure when reading that quote. You would need to possess strength in your voice, a flawless quality. You might not have the quality to deliver a read representing a broadcast network, but don't worry if you don't, there are many other types of reads and styles of voices needed, ones for which your voice will be perfect.

— Your attitude

Like anything you do in life it will involve interaction with people. People you like, people you might not care for. The voice-over industry is very small. Everybody knows everybody. Your reputation will follow you wherever you go, so govern yourself accordingly. Although some situations might require you to express yourself, it is best to keep a low profile. Try to get along with everybody, smile and do a good job. Your attitude is just as important to your success as is your talent.

— *It is a small business*

The voice-over business in reality is a small business. Everybody knows the best studios in which to record. Everyone is aware of certain talent who are famous for certain styles and reads. Word travels fast from coast to coast. As I inferred in the attitude section: the producer you worked with at a cable network yesterday could be head of promotion for a major TV network tomorrow. So, treat everyone with respect. Not only to preserve your reputation, but also, because it is the right way to work, and no past indiscretions will backfire on you in the future. The voice-over industry has a small business mentality. Remember that!

— *Your agent*

Your agent is your voice connection to big blue chip clients that you might never get your voice to, unless you know someone who sits on the board. Your agent's contacts will determine where and how far you will go. Just like any other profession. There are good agents, and there are bad ones. Some basic rules; never pay a fee and check out their reputations with outside sources. But, back to your agent relationship. Stay in touch with your agent! Network with him or her! Ask questions! They know what the market is demanding. You need to be in demand to get work. Keep them updated if you have perfected a new read style! Let them know your desires, and who you wish to work for. If I feel that I am not getting enough work, I will ask my agent; "Hey can we get a tape over to the promotion guy at HBO?" When I arrived at William Morris in New York, thanks to Billy Serow (he runs the voice-over division), I felt that I could pick up some more cable network business. One of my agents at William Morris is Mark Guss. He is very aggressive and reacts to the needs of his clients—a great characteristic in a voice-over agent. I told Mark I wanted to be on HBO. I expressed to him that I felt that my style fit their air style. Mark networked with producers at HBO on my behalf. Since then, I was hired to do a whole promo season of work for "The Chris Rock Show," "Jerry Seinfeld," "Tracey Takes On" and other ongoing work. He has also gotten me on ESPN, ESPN 2, The American Movie Classics Network, The WB Network, The Romance Channel and a great deal of other promo work. He listens, and he gets results. I stay in touch with my agent, and you need to do the same with your agents! It will have a positive effect on your career.

— *When your agent bolts*

If you do not rely on an agency or agent to get you work,

then this does not affect you, however if you are a signed talent...read on. When I was signed in 1993 to come to New York it was a risky move. After all, I was giving up a radio and voice-over career in South Florida that I had built up over the previous seven years. I was making great money and was established in that local market. To make that move was to give up a solid foundation with the hope of building a bigger one, but there were no guarantees of greater success. When you make a decision of this magnitude, you rely on your professional relationship with your agents to get you work. When one of them decides to move on, it sends shock tremors through your mind. "What do you mean you are leaving to become a publicist in Los Angeles? You are my agent! You convinced me to move to this big city! You are my motivator! My friend! You get me work! You talk to me when I'm down about not getting booked! You get me in to see the people I need to see! You got me all these big accounts! What now? What? What! What!!!" I know it is stressful. Your agent becomes your employer and when they walk away from you, it is like working for a company for tens years and then being told one morning that the company has just been sold. Then they say, "don't worry," the new owners are not going to make any changes. You get what I am saying. Agents do move around too, and they, too, are looking to move up or move out. So be prepared for the people you are comfortable with to move in and out of your career. You will be fine. It happened to me, and although it was a shock, I moved on and continued as I always did. Bottom line here is, if you are talented and determined, people will be interested in hiring you.

— *Marketing yourself*

If I had it my way, I would be the only client that my agents represent. The fact is that the agent that represents you is made up of a team. Usually three or four senior agents and their assistants. Those three or four agents are responsible for representing the whole roster of both male and female voice talent for the agency. Sometimes one person on the team is in charge of individually representing celebrities that also do voice-overs. So, you see, you are not the only person on your agent's mind. Your contract will dictate what you are, and what you are not, allowed to pursue on your own. Everyone works out their own contractual agreements and arrangements. But, if you can go after work on your own, or if you are living in Cleveland, Dallas, Cincinnati or any smaller market that does not require you to have agent representation, then you have to rely on your own marketing machine. Get agency and producer mailing lists. Stockpile their names and addresses on your computer. Keep your voice demo updated, and a good amount of cassettes stockpiled. Get a logo, print business cards, letterhead...Get organized! Look professional, and send those tapes out!

One of Sandy's dear radio friends, Freddie Cruz, the all night "Cruzer." Freddie's still one of South Florida's smoothest sounding radio de-jays. He can still be heard on air every night on Hot 105. Tune him in if you're down South.

Chapter 7

— Ongoing training

Do you think Tiger Woods doesn't take a lesson or two every once in a while or Mark McGwire doesn't get in the batting cage to practice hitting? Voice talent should be no different. Take a speech class! Work with a vocal coach! There are a multitude of ways to practice and modify your delivery and sound. Remember, your voice is your instrument, and hopefully, your source of income.

There are various people, mainly in major cities, that specialize in training actors, actresses and voice-over artists. You can use a teacher to lose a regional accent that might be hindering you in getting work. You might want to learn a dialect to increase your character voice range. You might want to learn how to attack words that are giving you a problem when reading copy. The english language is probably one of the hardest languages to speak. Its use of consonants and awkward sounds make it difficult to deliver in a smooth way, however, it will be your job to do so. These teachers will give you exercise copy to read, and they will help you train to accomplish your individual goals.

The cost of training with a vocal coach varies depending on how qualified they are and where that coach is located. I trained at New York Speech Improvement in New York City. Many famous actors and actresses go there to improve their voice or to work on dialects. Robert DeNiro trained there to learn his southern accent for the movie "Cape Fear." Their current rate is $100 an hour. Your work, and/or needs for improvement, would dictate how many hours you should invest. A pilot does not take one hour of flight time, then fly the plane. You should expect to go at least 10 hours in order to see some results.

— *ISDN*

Though I do not want to get into a long-winded discussion about the origin of digital transmission of audio (because it is not necessary for you to know that information) I will, however, brief you on the digital transmission of your voice and what the benefits mean to you as a voice talent. ISDN is a digital line provided by the phone company that is used to transmit information—your voice, computer related info, etc.—via a digital network. It makes it possible for you to be in a studio, say in New York City, and transmit your voice anywhere in the world in real time without any delay.

This technology which has been around for some time now enables you, as the voice talent, not to be bound by your geographic location. You could be a voice-over guy living in New Mexico, working with clients from Boston to Seattle, and never have to leave your New Mexico studio. Digital transmission...it is a beautiful thing! Analog technology, or if you will, "Ma" Bell's wires are here. So, call the phone company. Get an ISDN line installed and that's it? Sorry, there is more to do!

That ISDN line needs to network into a transmitter. There are various transmitting boxes; for example, Telos

Zephyr is one widely used by radio and TV stations across the country. These transmitting sources cost anywhere from $3,000-$5,000. Is that it? Uh, no! Sorry, you will also need recording equipment; a mic, a board...well, we will talk about setting up a home studio later. All you need to know for now is that the technology exists that enables you to be pretty much anywhere you want to be and still be able to work. For example, I was vacationing in South Florida. I had a commitment to work on a show called "Inside Stuff" for the National Basketball Association. As the in-show announcer, I was committed to two sessions a week. A Thursday half-hour day session, and a one-hour Friday night session that started late at night, around midnight, and ran about 45 minutes. When in town I would go to the NBA studios in Secaucus, New Jersey for the Thursday daytime session, and do the Friday late night session from my own home audio recording studio. Since my voice was identified with the image of the show, the producers prefer not to use fill-in voices. Of course, it spoils any plans of trying to get out-of-town if you have committed to a project like this. That is, unless you take advantage of ISDN. I found a studio in South Florida called Post Edge On South Beach. I set up the session time with the Florida studio. Engineering handled the technical issues. I did my session from South Beach at midnight and I was on the beach an hour later.

ISDN makes it possible for you to be where you want to be, and still send your voice where it needs to go.

— Promos

As I said earlier, promos are not commercials. They are promotional announcements, non-commercial, with the intention of promoting what is going on at the particular broadcast station where it is being aired. A promo can mature into a commercial as soon as the promotional source decides to take that promotional unit off its own air, and run it on another source. There is too much to try to teach you now. Rates vary depending on how much work you do, and who you are doing promos for. The promo business is very lucrative and has re-launched many voice over careers. With the onset and growth of cable there are many areas of opportunity for voice talent who want to do promos. Get in contact with promotion people at the places where you think you would be right, get your tape there or have your agent network on your behalf.

— The home recording studio

The home recording studio is an investment in your

talents. You could put an audio studio in your house with a cost ranging from $10,000 to $100,000. You want to stay with top of the line equipment, because voice-over industry standards are high. You also want your voice sounding the best it can, and good equipment will make a profound difference.

To inquire about a home studio you need to acquaint yourself with someone who has the knowledge and experience in building home studios. They will either tell you what to buy and charge you a consulting fee, or they can purchase your equipment and mark-up the price. You will then need a tech or engineer to install your studio. Unless you are a computer or audio geek, I do not advise you to set up your own new equipment in a test study to see if you qualify as a studio engineer.

— *Animation*

How many times have you watched a cartoon, and then ran around the house imitating Scooby Doo? Well, then, you are a nut! I do it all the time! Maybe you could do animation. Today's animation is not the same as yesterday's Warner Brothers characters, like Bugs Bunny and Porky Pig. Today the style is more of the natural sound with a character quality to your voice. Shows, like The Simpsons, display voices with a character edge. Mostly, all animation is originated and produced in Los Angeles. So, if you are not there, it is a pretty tough market to break into. Even having ISDN capabilities will not help. They want you there in the studio in person since you usually have to interact with other voice talent.

Animation originators, like Disney, usually rely on celebrity voice talents for their animation roles, but there is room for non-celebrity voice talents in this sector. So, if you want animation, move to Los Angeles, and get a very good agent! I am not saying that you cannot make it in animation if you are not in Los Angeles, it just increases your chances for success if you are there.

— *Movie trailers*

Like animation, most movie trailers are primarily produced where most of the major movie studios are located. You guessed it....Los Angeles. And, this sector of the voice-over business is the toughest to break into. A small percentage of voice-over people do the majority of the work. You will find trailer houses in and outside of Los Angeles. Most of the work is performed there, or the voice talent beam their voices there via ISDN. If you want to get, or feel you are right for this kind of work; then you need to send your demo reel, or have your agent forward your reel, to what they call trailer houses. They work for the movie studios producing movie trailers. Places like Aspect Ratio in Los Angeles. Ask your agent about pursuing this work on your behalf.

Movie trailer voices vary in style depending on the style of movie being promoted. They most often prefer the heavy deep voice, but the young hip sounding voice is "in" and will be used if that fits the appeal of the movie. There is room for all styles. Don Lon Fontaine and Hal Douglas are two of the leading trailer voices in America.

(l to r) Gordon Miller, MSNBC, Chief Audio Engineer; Sandy; and Steve Miller, Vice President of Advertising and Promotion, MSNBC.

Chapter 8

— *Working in the big three*

Success is nothing more than what you define it to be. I refer to it as one of those fake words. I mean that people generalize what success means, but really success is different things to different people. With reference to doing voice-over work, my illusion of success in this industry was to make it in New York; to perform national commercials for the biggest ad agencies in the entire world; and to have my voice promoting on the biggest, most notable networks. Work at the biggest studios, be involved with this industry at its highest level and make a really good living doing it.

Those were my goals. I have achieved all those goals. For me, success was making it in voice-overs in New York, one of the most competitive, fiercest voice-over markets in the world. Although I have not lived in Chicago or Los Angeles, I know those markets equal New York in the caliber of talent; size of the agencies and production companies; and, although there are some differences between these three major union voice-over markets, they also share many similarities.

Most of the big voice-over agencies have offices in all three cities. Most of the major advertising agencies also have offices in the big three, and the networks have studios in the three cities. I am not saying that agencies, producers, studios and companies are only in New York, Chicago and Los Angeles. I am saying that most of them are. There is work going on in a number of places like Miami, Dallas, Philadelphia, Boston, Houston, and other significant markets, like, Atlanta, San Francisco, Minneapolis and others.

I am focusing on New York since I work here, and it is a great market to look at when analyzing the voice-over industry at its highest most competitive level. All I can say is that if you are coming here with plans to make it in voice-overs, be prepared to work hard and understand that you are now functioning in one of the most talent filled voice-over markets in the world.

— *On hold*

If you are planning to work in New York, you are signed to an agent. If you are not, I suggest you make it your first priority. Like I said before, you have to audition to get work in New York, and the only way to get an audition is via a credible reputable agent. If you want a list of agents, pick up a *Ross Report*. You can find it at various book stores throughout the city. This is your industry reference guide. It lists agency names, agent names, what they do, addresses...you name it, it is in there. Get it! You need to have one.

Let's role play. Okay, you have your big time agent, you went on that audition and two days later the phone rings...it is your agent, he says, "Guess what?"

"Yeah?"

"You know that Campbell Soup audition you went on?"

"YEEEEAH?"

He says, "They want to put you on hold."

"YEEEEEEEEEEAHH!"

"Calm down, relax, relax," your agent says "its only a hold, man."

"Hold?" You say, "What in the world is a hold?"

Hold! It is when a client liked you for some reason, and they want to set your time aside on a certain day, or number of days, because they might (key word here, MIGHT) book you.

"So, I don't have the job yet?"

"Right!"

"No dollar signs yet?"

"Right."

"But why don't they make up their minds?"

Because they do not have to. Maybe it is between you and some one else. Maybe they are not sure if this campaign will meet with the approval of the client. It could be any number of a hundred reasons. Why? Don't ask why? Don't try to figure it out, just set the time aside if you have it available, be happy that someone noticed your voice and move on. Your agent will tell you when he or she will contact you as to the status of your hold.

— Released

If being told you are on hold brings your spirits up a bit. Being told you are released is the exact opposite. I mean, it is hard enough to get a job, to get that close, and then to be told, "thanks, but no thanks." It is enough to make you start bouncing off walls. And, believe me, I have done enough bouncing to get me to Calcutta. This is the nature of the business, folks. Welcome to big time voice-overs. Deal with it or be an accountant. Minds change, directions change, ideas come and go, people are on an account today, switched tomorrow. Do not try to figure it out, just know it is a part of the process. You will be put on hold. You will get that close to that six digit salary account! You will get that close to lotto! You will think of the money your going to make. Heck, you will have it spent in your head and then; "Sorry, they released you." I know it is hard, but do not start asking your agent: "But WHYYYYY? I was so good!" Are you kidding? Your agent has been giving this news to talent like you for years. He is like a doctor..."Sorry, Mrs. Jones, we tried everything possible to save him." You get the point! You are going to get dropped, it's part of the business. Accept it! Move on, because you will score that booking! You will! Hang in there!

— A booking

The phone rings! You are told it is your agent. A little adrenaline starts to pump. You wonder if one of those auditions you went on is finally going to pay off. Then you say to yourself, "No, I couldn't have gotten that Stouffer Hotel account, my agent said they cast that in New York, Los Angeles and Chicago, and every major voice in America was being heard. No, no way, not me."

You get the phone and say, "hi."

She says, "Guess what?"

"What?" You say.

"You got it."

"Got what?"

"The Stouffer Hotel account, you got it!!!"

"No way!!!"

"National network at double scale!!!"

That is the baseball equivalent of you hitting a grand slam in the bottom of the ninth at the world series in the seventh game with your team losing 5 to 2! Incidentally, that was a true story! It happened to me! It was my first booking through The Cunningham, Escott, Dipene Agency in New York. It was booked by my agent at the time, Diane Perez for the WYSE Advertising Agency in Cleveland. Those spots ran for three years and the residuals did not stop. It was at that point that I first really realized the potential of the industry that I was in, but I, also, knew that those days are far and few between. It would take a serious commitment on my part to sustain my career, support a family and live the life-style I had imagined. You will never forget your first booking, especially if it comes in at double scale.

— Losing that golden account

Voice-overs have a lot of similarities to life itself. Like life, the voice as a working tool is forever changing. Yeah, you could hold on to a voice-over account for 20 years, but that is rare. If your voice is on a campaign for a year, you should be ecstatic. You will lose accounts. And, the bigger the account, and the more money you are making from it; obviously, the more it will hurt when you lose it. You could be making over $200,000 a year from an account, and suddenly they decide it is time for a change. The creative team changes, they have new ideas and you are not a part of them. It happens, and it happens suddenly and coldly! Be prepared. Save some money, keep auditioning and keep moving forward. If you stay focused on the present, you will stay positive. If you live in a world of "what if," or "what could have been," you are going to be traveling on a long road. If you look back on your defeats too often, you tend to spiral down. Hey, I know it is hard. I lost an account on which I was making $60,000 a year. Boom, gone! $60,000 in income erased, and I was in the process of purchasing a house. Think I was stressed? But, I moved forward and a year later, after a year of using an on-camera celebrity, they came back and awarded the account back to me. Keep moving forward, and know that what comes to you, eventually goes away. It is a career you are focusing on. Go for the long term, not the short term!

— Negotiating a big time voice-over contract

Every voice talent dreams of getting a big voice-over deal. You know! A $150,000 deal to be the exclusive voice of a TV network, Cable network, or to be the voice of a major product. There are so many situations where a certain voice signs a six, or even, a seven figure deal in exchange for his, or her, voice to be one of the main image voices, or the main image voice, for a particular product. This is the lottery of voice-overs. It does happen. It is a combination of timing, talent and luck. I was fortunate enough to be chosen to be the network voice of the cable network, MSNBC. It requires me to be available to MSNBC daily. All deals are structured differently. Time frames, money, how much work to be performed are all points negotiated by you, your agent and your potential client.

Being flexible and open-minded are good traits to master when entering into a major negotiation with a big client. You should bounce your wants and needs off your agent. A reputable agent has negotiated many of these big time deals and knows what is fair and what is not. Rely on your representation, but be a part of the process. Read the finished contract before you sign it, and be comfortable with all the points you agreed to. This is your moment. Not many voice-over talent ever get offered that big contract. Be humble, and enjoy it! It might never come your way again.

Sandy in his recording studio in 1999.

1999. Doing a voice-over session for The E Channel. (l to r) Doug DiFranco, Engineer at McHale Barrone Studios, NY; Sandy; Mark Valentine, Director from Lee Hunt and Associates, NY; and Frank Brooks, Director of Creative Services for The E Channel.

Chapter 9

In This Chapter:

— Sessions
— Contracts
— Keeping records
— Good luck

— Sessions

Well, you finally scored a booking! You were booked on Thursday, at 10 a.m., to see so-and-so producer, from so-and-so big time Madison Avenue advertising agency, to be recorded at so-and-so big time recording studio uptown. A word of advice...do not be late! At $250, maybe more, an hour nobody needs to be waiting for you. Remember, you are not a star. You are a person that is lucky enough to possess, at this particular moment in time, a voice for which someone out there in creative land will compensate you. You provide one more spoke on the wheel. Producers want to get a great take of your voice into a digital work station, and move on to an edit, or whatever the next step in the creative process might be. Do not talk too much, but do not be afraid to be friendly. Balance your banter, but remember, you are there mainly to provide your voice as an instrument in a creative process. I do not mean to make this a cold process; however, it is a business and people are taking your performance very seriously. Everybody is on a tight schedule. The studio is booked. Another session is probably scheduled after yours, so, people cannot stop for small talk about what you did when you were in Bermuda. You will know if time allows for that. Just keep in mind why you are there.

— Contracts

If you are a non-union talent, then you are not dealing with AFTRA or SAG contracts. If you are, then you know you need to execute these contracts before you leave the session. They stipulate what you did, what union jurisdiction you performed them under, and they bind the client to compensate you for your performance. Make sure a contract is signed. Sometimes your agent receives your contract via a fax. Bottom line is that SAG & AFTRA contracts have to be executed by the producer, talent and signatory.

— *Keeping records*

You just opened your own small business and it is called, YOU. And like any business, you need a good record keeping system. Your agent, if you have one, will keep track of your jobs, process your payments, deduct their commission and, then, forward your compensation to you. But, it is important that you keep an accurate record of the jobs you performed, what you did at each job and when you did it. It is normal for certain clients to pay late and some to forget entirely. Your agent's accounts payable people are tracking talent payments for hundreds of talent; so information can, and does, fall through the cracks. You need to keep track of your own accounts receivables. This way you can keep up with late, and outstanding, monies owed to you. You will ultimately remind your agent about jobs that have not been paid. Do not expect her, or him, to remember. It will happen! It has happened to me hundreds of times, and I mean that literally...hundreds! Keep track! Get a file cabinet and a computer. Log your jobs and keep all your scripts. You might need them three months from now to prove that you did the job. But, do not worry, you will get paid. If you are not union, then, you are going to be doing all your own invoicing and collecting. I am sure that I do not need to tell you to have an accurate reliable record keeping system. Treat your voice-over career as you would a small business. Have a filing system. Keeping records will keep you organized, and keep you from losing money that is owed to you.

— Good luck

Well, this concludes my tour of the world of voice-overs. I hope I have given you some insight into what goes on there, and you feel that you are one step closer to knowing what you need to know. Maybe you want to go further, maybe I scared you away. I tried to be accurate. Although, at times you might have felt that my words were pessimistic in nature, they were meant to give you only the raw truth about this business. Voice-overs is a wonderful way to make a living. Hey, what could be better than making your own hours, answering to, literally, no one and making lots of money in very little time. You couldn't imagine a better job! It is just that this field is fiercely competitive, and not many people make it to the top dollar jobs, and to leave out that perspective from this book would be unfair to any reader. So that I can leave you on an up note, I will relate my own experience. As a boy who grew up in New York, I was as unlikely to make it in this industry as anybody would have been. I had a horrible, thick regional accent, and was not gifted with an incredible voice. I am an example of the philosophy that if you want it badly enough, and are willing to work at it, you will get there and succeed. From a guy who made it in this crazy field, I say to you, much success, best of luck and remember to laugh a lot! Laugh...it is only a voice-over.

Sandy at the NBA Studios in New Jersey in 1999 doing voice work for the NBA show called "Inside Stuff."

Sample Scripts

The following pages contain commercial and promo copy that I voiced, they are here for you to practice your read styles. You will notice that the caption will designate the type of category that the script represents. Example: Hotel/Resort commercial copy category or network news copy category. You will also notice on some that the client name has been omitted. When you come to this omitted place you will see "Client." At that place, you fill in a client name of your choice. For example, if it is a restaurant script, fill in the client with a name like Friday's or Bennigan's. If you are reading a hotel script fill in the client name with a hotel name like Hilton or Marriott. Use whatever you feel like using. The name is unimportant, you are just trying to practice getting through the copy smoothly.

Remember, this is just an exercise. These scripts are intended to introduce you to what you will be reading in the voice-over industry at bookings and auditions. Get your tape recorder out, and record yourself reading these scripts. Listen back. Play your reads for other people and get some feedback. Does it sound smooth or awkward? Are you having trouble reading through the copy or pronouncing certain words?

This is an exercise meant to familiarize you with reading commercial and promotional copy. What you hear back on the tape might please or displease you. Do not worry about your performance at this time, when you begin training with a teacher or enroll in a voice-over class you will be taught techniques on how to improve and master reading copy. Look at this as a practice session.

(l to r) At MSNBC to record with avid editor Barry Spitzer; Assistant Audio Engineer, Eric Casimiro; MSNBC Producer, Michael Weingartner; Sandy; and Chief Audio Engineer, Gordon Miller in 1999.

SPORTING GOODS STORE
COMMERCIAL COPY CATEGORY

(Fill in client name with the name of a sporting goods store that you know)

BACK TO SCHOOL 2
:60 RADIO, VERSION 2
No tags

(SFX: ANNCR. REPEATS NAMES)
Nike. Reebok. Jansport. Nike. Reebok. Jansport.

ANNCR: (CLIENT) would like to remind you that there are only three names you really need to know to get ready for school.

(SFX: ANNOUNCER'S VOICE COMES UP FROM UNDERNEATH, THEN FADES AGAIN):
"Nike. Reebok. Jansport."

Remember these names from now until September 6th and you'll really look smart because (CLIENT) is having a Back To School Sale with incredible savings.

(SFX: NAMES FADE, MUSIC UP AND UNDER)

Men, strut in on your first day back in Reebok D Factor basketball, Nike basketball or Reebok Eliminator Cross-training shoes for just 49.99!

And women, slip on a pair of Nike Runner Classics for 34.99, Reebok Weathermax walking shoes just 49.99 or Nike Air-trainer Circuit Lo's, only 57.59.

Find a better deal advertised anywhere else, and we'll match that price. It's called (CLIENT)'s New Price Protection Policy, and it guarantees the best price on everything we carry. Now that's what we call being competitive.

Come into (CLIENT)'s now, and you'll also find Jansport Classic Day Packs, you know, the cool kind with the leather bottom, for just 29.99.

(MUSIC FADES, NAMES UP AND UNDER)

So don't forget those three magic words.
Nike Reebok Jansport

(SFX: ANNCR. CHANGES HYPNOTIC REPETITION OF BRAND NAMES TO:)
        "(CLIENT) Back To School Sale."

Okay. Five words. It's good you know your math!

LONG DISTANCE CARRIER
COMMERCIAL COPY CATEGORY

(Fill in client name with a long distance carrier like AT&T, Sprint or MCI)

Finally, your Internet is ready.

With (CLIENT) you can e-mail friends

Or chat and make some new ones.

Surf the Web.

There's even child safety software.

And your own personal sign-up page.

All for just $14.95 a month.

And if you call now, you can get up to...

10 of the latest software titles free.

So call now.

Call now for the fast easy way onto the Internet.

CABLE TV
PROMO COPY CATEGORY

DESTINATION WEDNESDAY

WHERE
ARE
YOU
GOING?

ISN'T IT TIME YOU HAD A DESTINATION-
A PLACE TO FIND THE BEST ORIGINAL SERIES ON TV-

ALL ON ONE NIGHT.
IT'S "DESTINATION WEDNESDAY,"

PRIMETIME HBO.
BE THERE AT 8 PM,

STARTING WITH "ARLISS"-
WHERE AMERICA'S SUPER AGENT
DRIVES HOME THE BIGGEST DEALS IN SPORTS

AND THEN THERE'S "SEX AND THE CITY"-
WHERE WOMEN TAKE THE LEAD AND RELATIONSHIPS RULE

FOLLOWED BY "THE SOPRANOS,"
WHERE A "FAMILY" WILL DRIVE YOU INSANE

AND WATCH OUT—YOU'RE IN "OZ"...
IT'S NO PLACE LIKE HOME

THEN MEET UP WITH TODD McFARLANE'S "SPAWN"...
AND SEE THE FORCES OF GOOD AND EVIL COLLIDE

DESTINATION WEDNESDAY.
IT'S ALL ORIGINAL AND IT'S RIGHT HERE.

EVERY WEDNESDAY NIGHT AT 8,
BEGINNING JUNE 6th...
OVER 3 HOURS OF PRIME HBO SERIES.

FINALLY...
YOU'VE ARRIVED.

(TAGS)
EVERY WEDNESDAY NIGHT STARTING AT 8
OVER 3 HOURS OF PRIME HBO SERIES.

TONIGHT STARTING AT 8
OVER 3 HOURS OF PRIME HBO SERIES.

LOCAL RADIO
PROMO COPY CATEGORY

—IF IT ROCKS. IT'S PURE ROCK. LAZER 103.3.

—*(sketch out)* MANCOW. *(back to normal read)* THERE'S ONLY ONE PLACE TO GET YOUR MANCOW FIX. PURE ROCK LAZER 103.3.

—THE MANCOW MILLENNIUM IS COMING. (sbt) MANCOW'S MORNING MADHOUSE, EVERY MORNING, ON PURE ROCK LAZER 103.3.

—IF YOU DIDN'T KNOW, THAT'S OUR WEBSITE. LAZER 1033.COM! TAKE A BREAK FROM THE PORN SITES AND GET CAUGHT UP ON WHAT'S HAPPENING IN THE WORLD OF LAZER. PURE ROCK ON THE WORLD WIDE WEB. LAZER 1033.COM!

—WANNA CATCH A BUZZ? (sbt) IT'S LAZER 103.3'S BUZZ CUT.

—LOCKED ONTO A 103 MINUTE PURE ROCK BLOCK. NON STOP PURE ROCK. LAZER 103.3!

YOU'RE IN THE MIDDLE OF A 103 MINUTE PURE ROCK BLOCK. SO GET ROCKED. OR GET OUT OF THE WAY. LAZER 103.3!

—CRACKIN' OPEN A CAN OF WOOP ASS! IT'S A LAZER 103.3. 103 MINUTE PURE ROCK BLOCK. AND IT STARTS ...NOW!

—IT'S TIME TO BRING THE NOISE! KICKIN' OFF ANOTHER 103 MINUTE PURE ROCK BLOCK!

—IF IT ROCKS, IT'S PURE ROCK. AND THIS IS A 103 MINUTE PURE ROCK BLOCK. ONLY ON LAZER 103.3!

—READY TO ROCK? KICKIN' OFF A PURE ROCK BLOCK..ON LAZER 103.3. BIGGER IS BETTER!

—LAZER 103.3 BRINGS YOU (sbt) ANOTHER PURE ROCK BLOCK!

—WHEN IT COMES TO ROCKIN' OUT...SIZE DOES MATTER! AND NO ONE ELSE ON THE DIAL MEASURES UP TO LAZER 103.3 103 MINUTE PURE ROCK BLOCKS! BIGGER. BETTER. LONGER. STRONGER. LAZER 103.3 103 MINUTE PURE ROCK BLOCKS. THE. MOST. NON. STOP. ROCK. IN DES MOINE!

FURNITURE MANUFACTURER
COMMERCIAL COPY CATEGORY

(Fill in client name with the name of a furniture manufacturer that you know)

ANNCR: Most people come here to see the sights...the big farms and rolling hills, the black buggies and little girls in sun bonnets. But when (CLIENT) furniture comes to Amish country, it's strictly business. Talk about board feet of lumber and dovetail joints...with the serious men in the big black beards...who build the (CLIENT) Furniture Timber Mill collection. Designed by (CLIENT). Built by the Amish. With clean, honest lines, Shaker-simple design. Chests of drawers, bookcases, a desk as delicate as air. All made of fine-grained wild American black cherry that ages and darkens to a rich copper color...it's oil finish hand-rubbed satin-smooth...And all of it built so well, it's as close as anything in life comes...to being forever. The (CLIENT) Furniture Timber Mill Collection. Designed right. Built right. Priced right.

FURNITURE MANUFACTURER
COMMERCIAL COPY CATEGORY

(Fill in client name with the name of a furniture manufacturer that you know)

ANNCR: We found the first one in an old farmhouse in Tuscany. A pine armoire...six feet high, with a beautiful, graceful arched top...it was <u>more</u> than charming...it was love at first sight. We bought that beautiful pine armoire on the spot and had it shipped home to <u>(CLIENT)</u> <u>furniture</u>. And the day it arrived, we ripped it apart. And set our <u>own Amish craftsmen</u> to work...building an armoire that looked like this one...but was made the (CLIENT) way. We used the finest northern American pine. Gave it two coats of beeswax <u>finish</u>, hand-rubbed to a rich honey color.

(BUILD)
So now, you can come, to (CLIENT) furniture and buy an Italian armoire...made of American pine, by Amish craftsmen in Ohio...that looks just like an authentic European antique.

The (CLIENT) furniture pine armoire. Designed right. Built right. Priced right.

CABLE TV
PROMO COPY CATEGORY

(Fill in client name with the name of a cable TV channel that you know)

ANNCR: TONIGHT, YOU CAN GET UNDER THE COVERS

(SFX: WAR SOUNDS)

ANNCR: OR YOU CAN <u>TAKE</u> COVER.

RELIVE THE GREATEST TANK BATTLES IN HISTORY—FROM THE SANDS OF AFGHANISTAN TO THE FIELDS OF KUWAIT-THROUGH THE EYES OF THOSE WHO FOUGHT AND SURVIVED.

THEN, RIDE IN THE COCKPIT OF A STEALTH BOMBER, LAND AN APACHE HELICOPTER AND EXPERIENCE FIRING AN ANTI-TANK MISSILE ALL FROM THE COMFORT OF YOUR FAVORITE CHAIR.

IT'S AMAZING WHAT YOU'LL DISCOVER WHEN YOU TUNE IN LATE. FIELDS OF ARMOR & FIRE POWER STARTING AT MIDNIGHT ON THE (CLIENT) CHANNEL. TONIGHT.

CABLE TV
PROMO COPY CATEGORY

(Fill in client name with the name of a cable TV channel that you know)

Keyable graphic:
> *"TONIGHT, YOU CAN..." over sleep footage.*

ANNCR: TONIGHT YOU CAN SLIP INTO A DEEP SLEEP...

Keyable graphic:
> *"OR..."*

over exciting Secrets of the Deep footage.

ANNCR: OR PLUNGE INTO A DEEP DIVE.

(CONTINUES)

EXPLORE THE ICY WATERS OF PATOGONIA, DESCEND TO THE REMAINS OF A CIVIL WAR BATTLESHIP, SWIM WITH THE GREAT WHITE, SEARCH FOR THE LOST CITY OF ATLANTIS, SCUBA TO THE ENDS OF THE EARTH AND UNLOCK THE SECRETS OF THE DEEP.

IT'S AMAZING WHAT YOU'LL DISCOVER WHEN YOU TUNE IN LATE. SECRETS OF THE DEEP AT MIDNIGHT ON THE (CLIENT) CHANNEL. TONIGHT!

CABLE TV
PROMO COPY CATEGORY

(Fill in client name with the name of a cable TV channel that you know)

ANNCR: TONIGHT, YOU CAN FALL ASLEEP...
OR FALL FORTY STORIES.

(CONTINUES)

FROM DEEP SPACE NINE TO STAR TREK. FROM CLIFFHANGER TO JURASSIC PARK. GO BEHIND THE SCENES AS DISCOVERY REVEALS THE SECRETS OF HOLLYWOOD'S SPECIAL EFFECTS.

THEN, WHEN A COMPUTER CRASHES, WHAT HAS IT HIT? HOW DOES A SQUASH MAKE AN ENGINE RUN BETTER? WHAT IS THE SECRET LIFE OF MACHINES?

IT'S AMAZING WHAT YOU'LL DISCOVER WHEN YOU <u>TUNE</u> IN LATE. THE SECRET LIFE OF MACHINES AT MIDNIGHT ON THE (CLIENT) CHANNEL. TONIGHT!

Sandy Thomas and Gordon Miller, Chief Audio Engineer, on the set at MSNBC in April of 1999.

CABLE TV
PROMO COPY CATEGORY

(Fill in client name with the name of a cable TV channel that you know)

Keyable graphic:
   "TONIGHT, YOU CAN..."
over sleeping footage.

      ANNCR: TONIGHT, YOU CAN CATCH FORTY WINKS...

Keyable graphic:
   "OR..."
over exciting Wings of the Red Star footage.

      ANNCR: OR PURSUE MIG 21'S

(CONTINUES)

THEY <u>OUTPACED</u> WESTERN TECHNOLOGY FOR <u>FIFTY YEARS</u>, DEVAST<u>ATING</u> THEIR OPPONENTS IN <u>KOREA</u>, <u>ISRAEL</u> AND <u>AFGHANISTAN</u>. EXPERIENCE THE INCREDIBLE AND <u>OFTEN</u> <u>ASTOUNDING</u> ACHIEVEMENTS OF THE SOVIET <u>AIR</u> FORCE. FROM THE FIRST SUPERSONIC BOMBER TO THE FINAL ATTACK <u>HELICOPTERS</u>.

IT'S <u>AMAZING</u> WHAT YOU'LL <u>DISCOVER</u> WHEN YOU TUNE IN LATE. <u>WINGS OF THE RED STAR</u> AT <u>MIDNIGHT</u> ON THE <u>(CLIENT)</u> CHANNEL. TONIGHT!

MUSIC ARTIST
COMMERCIAL COPY CATEGORY

MUSIC: *I Still Believe, When You Believe (From The Prince of Egypt), Honey*

VO: One extraordinary new album

VO: Mariah Carey, #1's.

SUPER: *Mariah Carey, #1's.*

SUPER: *Vision of Love, Emotions, Hero, One Sweet Day, My All, and more.*

VO: Celebrating 13 record-breaking #1 singles plus 4 new bonus tracks. Featuring the new single I Still Believe and When You Believe (From The Prince Of Egypt), the landmark duet with Whitney Houston.

ALT VO: Featuring When You Believe (From The Prince Of Egypt), the landmark duet with Whitney Houston and the new single I Still Believe.

VO: Mariah #1's.
In stores now.

HOTEL
COMMERCIAL COPY CATEGORY

(Fill in client name with the name of a hotel that you know)

On Mexico City TV

Anncr VO:

There are all kinds of places to go in Mexico City.

But only one place to stay.

Because there's no hotel in Mexico City quite like the (CLIENT)

With quite the sophistication.

Quite the style.

Quite the support for business.

The (CLIENT).

There's nothing quite like it in Mexico City.

NETWORK NEWS
PROMO COPY CATEGORY

(Fill in client name with the name of a news channel that you know)

((YOUR READ))

TONIGHT ON (CLIENT)

SERBS SAY NATO BOMBS KILLED 100 REFUGEES IN KOSOVO. BUT IS NATO RESPONSIBLE? DID THEY MAKE ANOTHER DEADLY MISTAKE?

AND, (ANY FEMALE NAME) SPEAKS OUT ABOUT THE PRESIDENT, THE ALLEGED GROPING INCIDENT, AND THE THREATS SHE SAYS WERE MADE AGAINST HER.

NEXT ON (CLIENT)

NETWORK NEWS
PROMO COPY CATEGORY

(Fill in client name with the name of a news channel that you know)

((YOUR READ))

Behind in the polls & distrusted by his own party Al Gore is out to re-invent himself

But will the make-over come in time

On the News with Brian Williams tomorrow at 9 Eastern on (CLIENT)

Tonight at 9 Eastern on (CLIENT)

Next on (CLIENT)

NETWORK NEWS
PROMO COPY CATEGORY

(Fill in client name with the name of a news channel that you know)

TOUGH QUESTIONS
—jk sot—"who else is liable"

BIG CASES
—da sot—"there's gotta be some accountability here."

((YOUR READ))

YOUR CHANCE TO PUT OUR LEGAL SYSTEM ON TRIAL.
JUDGE AND JURY WEEKDAYS NOON EASTERN ON MSNBC.

(TAGS)

TODAY NOON EASTERN ON (CLIENT)

NEXT ON (CLIENT)

LOCAL RADIO
PROMO COPY CATEGORY

((YOUR READ))

JUNE 12, LIVE AT DODGER STADIUM-IT'S
THE WILD, WILD WANGO TANGO TWO.
RICKY MARTIN, WILL SMITH, BLONDIE,
SHAGGY, 98 DEGREES AND BRITNEY SPEARS.
TICKETS ON SALE SATURDAY
TICKETS ON SALE NOW

UB40
ENRIQUE IGLESIAS
DRU HILL
IN CONCERT

PRESENTED BY PEPSI-THE JOY OF COLA AND
THE RIO SUITE HOTEL AND CASINO.

(TAGS)

TICKETS ON SALE SATURDAY FROM TICKETMASTER

TICKETS ON SALE NOW FROM TICKETMASTER

LOCAL RADIO
PROMO COPY CATEGORY

WANGO TANGO II PROMO-WTII1

((YOUR READ))

KIIS TURNS ON SUMMER WITH RICKY MARTIN...
KIIS TURNS ON SUMMER WITH WILL SMITH...

THE WILD...WILD...WANGO...TANGO...TWO.

PLUS WILL SMITH
PLUS RICKY MARTIN
BRITNEY SPEARS, 98 DEGREES, ENRIQUE IGLESIAS,
DRU HILL, SHAGGY...AND BLONDIE.

SATURDAY-JUNE 12-DODGER STADIUM

TICKETS ARE ON SALE SATURDAY
BUT IF YOU WAIT...YOU LOSE.
GET TO A TICKETMASTER LOCATION QUICK
OR CALL 213-480-3232.

*(TAGS)**

*TICKETS ARE ON SALE TOMORROW...

*TICKETS ARE ON SALE NOW...

THE WILD, WILD WANGO TANGO TWO FROM PEPSI-THE JOY OF COLA AND THE RIO SUITE HOTEL AND CASINO. WITH PART PROCEEDS GOING TO RONALD McDONALD HOUSE AND CHARITIES OF SOUTHERN CALIFORNIA.

ONE CONCERT...ONE DAY...ONE STATION...

102.7 KIIS FM

FAST FOOD PIZZA DELIVERY
COMMERCIAL COPY CATEGORY

(Fill in client name with the name of a fast food pizza place that you know)

SFX: *Guy on phone with wife. Dog barking. Cat hissing. Kids screaming.*

GUY: Yeah, everything's fine, honey. We're doing great. I love you, too.

SFX: *Doorbell rings. Dog barks.*

GUY: Oooops, gotta get the door. See you soon. (pause) Be right there.

SFX: *Door opens.*

YOU (PIZZA GUY):   (CLIENT) Delivery.

GUY: Oh, great. Thanks.

SFX: *Door closes.*

SFX: *Doorbell rings. Dog barks.*

GUY: Hold on, hold on.

SFX: *Door opens.*

YOU (PIZZA GUY):   Your second pizza, sir.

GUY: Wow, I get two pizzas. Cool.

SFX: *Door closes.*

SFX: *Doorbell rings. Dog barks.*

GUY: Boy, I'm popular today.

SFX: *Door opens.*

YOU (PIZZA GUY):   Your salad, sir.

GUY: Thanks again.

SFX: *Door closes.*

SFX: *Doorbell rings. Dog barks.*

GUY: What now?

SFX: *Door opening.*

YOU (PIZZA GUY):   Your chocolate chip cookies, sir.

GUY: (incredulous) Oh, yeah, the chocolate chip cookies. How could I forget?

ANNCR: Introducing the new (CLIENT) "Dinner for Four". For just $13.99, get two medium, one-topping pizzas, garden salad for four—with choice of dressing. And for dessert, 4 chocolate chip cookies. All this, for just $13.99. Offer available for delivery and carryout only. For a limited time at participating restaurants and delivery units. Limited delivery areas.

SFX: *Doorbell rings. Dog barks.*

GUY: Seems like I've done this before.

SFX: *Door opens.*

YOU (PIZZA GUY):   Uh, sir, that'll be $13.99?

SFX: *Dog growls.*

NATIONAL CHAIN RESTAURANT COMMERCIAL COPY CATEGORY

(Fill in client name with the name of a national restaurant chain that you know)

SFX: HIGH SPEED VEHICLES, TV THEME MUSIC THROUGHOUT. GLADYS AND JIM ARE ROADSIDE OBSERVERS.

JIM: Used to be one or two cars a day came by.

GLADYS: Now even the chickens won't cross the road.

ANNCR (YOU): If you're not already on your way to (CLIENT) better find a shortcut fast.

GLADYS: What's all the hurry for?

ANNCR (YOU): (CLIENT) Santa Fe Fajita Feast is off and running. And the special price-just $11.95 on Fajitas for Two-can't last forever.

DRIVER: (SCREECHING BRAKES) Quick-which way to (CLIENT)'s?

JIM: Well, let's see...

DRIVER: Can't wait. I'll find it.
(SQUEALING TIRES).

ANNCR (YOU): Now a quick trip to (CLIENT) lands you in the southwest for the authentic taste of Santa Fe fajitas. Charbroiled strips of tender chicken and beef, piled with sizzling peppers and onions. And real Santa Fe tortillas. More than enough for two for just $11.95.

So put it in gear.

And, once you've raced over to (CLIENT) try their other southwest treats like nachos and quesadillas. Go ahead. You just saved plenty on those $11.95 Fajitas for Two.

JIM: Better get going, huh?

GLADYS: I'm taillights.
(MOTORCYCLE ENGINE. SQUEALING TIRES).

ANNCR (YOU): The southwest is waiting at (CLIENT). And Fajitas for Two are just $11.95. So hurry. (CLIENT) Santa Fe Fajita Feast comes to an abrupt stop soon. *(BRAKES SCREECH).*

CABLE TV
PROMO COPY CATEGORY

(They are looking for a natural sound–not overly broadcasty–a casual, but friendly, voice that can carry authority through a cluttered spot. Must be able to deliver comedy by bringing humor and spice to the scripts.)

(Nick at Nite Instant Gratification Tune In
Writer: Tom Hill, Nancy Kirwan, David Rieth   Producer: Mark King
Length: 30)

There's nothing worse than watching a great episode when suddenly....*(music: dun dun dun!)*

Graphic: "To be Continued"

That's why Nick at Nite puts those multi-part episodes together for you every Sunday nite. See two parters...back to back. Three parters...back to back to back.

That's Instant Gratification Sundays.

You get all the plot twists and big stories—without those "to be continued blues!"

Get TV Hits from Nick at Nite! Now in convenient Instant Gratification Sundays, every Sunday staring at 9/8 central.

CABLE TV
PROMO COPY CATEGORY

Monuments of natural splendor.

Symbols of freedom.

Triumphs of design and ingenuity.

These are the artifacts that mark our nations past, and help direct us into the future.

Join The History Channel as we look at the stories behind these national treasures, and examine the on going efforts to preserve them for future generations.

For information on how you can help Save our History call 888-87-Learn.

Save our history with The History Channel

CABLE TV
PROMO COPY CATEGORY

(Fill in client name with the name of a cable TV channel that you know)

BEST OF TLC—RADIO COPY

ANNCR (YOU):   Are you tired of other people always saying what's best for you? I mean like *(CHANGES VOICE)* "Larry you're a great guy...but I think it's best if we don't see each other for a while." Or when you hear, *(TOUGH)* Buddy, I think it's best if you come downtown with us..." Or your mom saying, *(CHANGES VOICE)* Dear, you know cod liver oil's best for that upset stomach." Or some sales guy saying *(CHANGES VOICE)* "I'm telling you, m'am, this do-it-yourself lyposuction kit is the best thing since sliced bread!" Well, you know what's best for you, right? And now, TLC presents an action-packed week of television that you think is best...The Best of TLC Week—The year's most revealing adventures for your mind...chosen by the people who know us...best...Our viewers.

SFX: *HEART MONITOR CROSS FADE TO*

ANNCR (YOU):   From the best real life emergency room dramas...and medical breakthroughs...

SFX: *JACKHAMMER CROSS FADE TO*

ANNCR (YOU):   ...to the best and biggest things ever built...

SFX: *WEDDING MARCH CROSS FADERS TO*

ANNCR (YOU):	From the best look ever at human mating rituals...
SFX:	*COWBOYS WHOOPING IT UP*
ANNCR (YOU):	To the best of the old west at its wildest...
SFX:	*THUNDERCLAP/WIND CROSS FADE TO*
ANNCR (YOU):	...and Mother Nature at her worst...
MUSIC:	*HIT AND GO*
ANNCR (YOU):	The Best of TLC Week...All your favorite shows of 1998...All packed into one powerful week of television. All on TLC...starting Sunday night at eight eastern and pacific. The best adventures for your mind.

RESTAURANT
COMMERCIAL COPY CATEGORY

(Fill in client name with the name of a restaurant that you know)

Ever wonder why New Yorkers have big mouths?

Because we eat big pizza. Like the Big New Yorker from (CLIENT).

Eight big foldable slices of real street corner pizza at a price that's very un-New York.

The Big New Yorker, new from (CLIENT).

RACING
COMMERCIAL COPY CATEGORY

NASCAR
:30
3/5/99

(Avo)

What's the next best thing to racing for the Winston Cup? Downshifting to NASCAR-online.

Log on anytime and get all the latest news, up-to-the-second standings and in-depth track analysis.

Plus GarageCam shows you how your favorite crew and driver are gearing up for the weekend.

And during the race, find out instantly your favorite driver's position and how the track's running.

You can even listen in as drivers radio to their pit crew live.

(Natural Sound: Motortrax)

When the green flag drops, strap in to the official site of NASCAR-NASCAR.com. To get any deeper into the race, you'd have to qualify.

SPORTS
PROMO COPY CATEGORY

IN HIS 10 YEAR CAREER HE HAS MISSED ONLY ONE GAME AND THE ONLY THING GREATER THAN HIS TALENT IS HIS HEART, HIS UNQUESTIONED OBEDIENCE TO THE GOD OF GUTS.

AS PAYTON PUTS IT-"THERE'S A VOICE INSIDE ME SAYING, 'YOU CAN ALWAYS DO BETTER.'"-TO KNOW THE POWER OF THAT VOICE IS TO SEE WALTER PAYTON BATTLE THROUGH A BROKEN FIELD.

ON THE ROAD TO SUPER BOWL 19 PAYTON LED THE BEARS TO THE DIVISION CHAMPIONSHIP AND ALONG THE WAY KEPT AN APPOINTMENT WITH DESTINY.

PAYTON'S REMARKABLE RECORD WAS EQUALED ONLY BY THE SPIRIT IN WHICH IT WAS ACHIEVED, WALTER PAYTON-A PROUD MEMBER OF A UNIQUE FRATERNITY OF FIGHTING MEN AND A PLAYER WHO HAS ALWAYS TRAVELED THE PATHS OF GLORY.

BEER
COMMERCIAL COPY CATEGORY

(Fill in client name with the name of a beer that you know)

OPEN:

This is Brad Nickerson, guitar craftsman. He builds quality guitars by hand. When he's done for the day, he loves the sound of a well-built beer *(SFX: beer opening)*. (CLIENT).

CLOSE:

Brought to you by (CLIENT) a well-built beer. (CLIENT) Ale Brewing Company. Portsmouth, New Hampshire. Thanks for doing it right, Brad.

BEER
COMMERCIAL COPY CATEGORY

(Fill in client name with the name of a beer that you know)

OPEN:

Roger Hopkins builds walls...the kind they write about. When his day's done he reaches for something just as solid *(SFX: Beer opening)* the taste of a well-built beer, (CLIENT).

CLOSE:

Brought to you by (CLIENT) a well-built beer (CLIENT) Ale Brewing Company. Portsmouth, New Hampshire. Thanks, Roger.

BEER
COMMERCIAL COPY CATEGORY

(Fill in client name with the name of a beer that you know)

OPEN:

Here's Robbin and Jules, log home builders. They do things perfectly and by hand. And when the work's done, *(SFX: Beer opening)* they go for the taste of a well-built beer (CLIENT).

CLOSE:

Brought to you by (CLIENT) a well-built beer. (CLIENT) Ale Brewing Company. Portsmouth, New Hampshire. Thanks, guys.

Sandy and his Dad, Eddie.

Exhibits & References

Pay stub from voice work Sandy did for Adidas. This is a residual payment.

AD AGY/PROD CO													
TEAM ONE ADVERTISING			**TELA**										

COMMERCIAL ID -
ADDR3600
ORIGINAL ID -
EDIT VERSION:

ADVERTISER
ADIDAS
PRODUCT **BASKETBALL SHOES**

TITLE
SPORTSCASTER
UNION **AFTMIA** DATE 1ST SERVICE **6 03 93** YEAR CODE **91** CATE GORY **ANN** CAP ERA **OFF** DOUBLING OVERSCALE **1 0** SESSION INFORMATION

FIRST NO DATE **6 15 93** FIRST FIXED CYCLE **3 02 95** MAXIMUM PERIOD OF USE A F M CONTRACT REG A F M LEADER A F S7 DUR DATE OVERTIME HRS 1½ X 2X

MADE FOR CABLE ONLY
RADIO REUSE HTLDEPOT
USAGE TYPE USE WHD **1 3** # HUM **1 0** CYCLE DATES **1 0 93** TO **1 11 34**

MADE FOR SPANISH
CLASS & USE DATES / / / / / / / /
/ / / / / / / /
TRAVEL HOURS PRIOR FIT HOURS
INCLUDE

WILD SPOT INITIAL WILD SPOT UPGRADE TO / / / / / / /
MAJOR CITIES PLUS UNITS **47** MAJOR CITIES PLUS UNITS AMOUNT APPLIED CAN TAX INVOICE NO **K30172** SPOTS TAGS

COMMENTS

INQUIRIES TO
EMPLOYER OF RECORD FOR WITHHOLDING AND UNEMPLOYMENT (U C) INSURANCE IS

EMPLOYEE NAME
SANTO CASTELLANO
CHECK NUMBER **06665719**
RESIDENCE STATE **NY** STATE WORKED **FL** AGENT CODE **0162** PAY ENDING MO **11** DAY **04** YR **93**

SOCIAL SECURITY NO FEDERAL I D. NO CORPORATION FSO STATE U C **1184182**

GROSS EARNINGS	MISC PAYMENTS	REIMBURS EXP	MONIES DUE TP THIS PAY	TAXABLE EARNINGS THIS PAY	TOTAL DEDUCTIONS	TAX LIENS GARNISHMENTS	AMOUNT OF CHECK
29931				**29931**	**5373**		**24558**

FED W/H TAX	FICA	STATE TAX	RESIDENCE STATE TAX	SUI	LOCAL TAX	CANADIAN TAX	MISC. DED	STATE DISABILITY
3083	**2290**	:	:	:	:			:

YEAR TO DATE TOTALS GROSS EARNINGS	MISC. PAYMENTS	REIMBURSEMENT EXP	FED W/H TAX	FICA	STATE TAX	LOCAL TAX	CANADIAN TAX
482439	**000**	**5073**	**51634**	**36907**	:	:	:

Sandy was chosen as the voice to launch the network, ESPN 2. The following are AFTRA contracts from two of those voice-over sessions: This contract was for a radio session.

RADIO PROGRAMS   and   AFTRA   H&R REMITTANCE REPORT;PRODUCTION REPORT

Live Commercials   Network or Local Broadcast

IMPORTANT ⇒ Make checks payable to AFTRA HEALTH AND RETIREMENT FUNDS and mail this report to the H&R office in New York, Chicago, or Los Angeles (address below) depending on city in which radio programs covered by this report are made. If city other than New York, Chicago or Los Angeles, contact the local AFTRA office for information. Use this form for live or recorded programs, including repeats or re-plays, and live commercials.

260 MADISON AVENUE, NEW YORK 10016   307 N. MICHIGAN AVE., CHICAGO 60601   6922 HOLLYWOOD BLVD., HOLLYWOOD 90028

HEALTH and RETIREMENT

Reporting Co. _Lee Hunt Associates_
73 Spring St
Address _NYC 10012_

Account No. _38012_ Date _9.30.93_
Signature _Lee Hunt Soll_
This sheet is page _1_ of _1_ pages.
(Use additional sheets if more space needed)

HEALTH AND RETIREMENT REMITTANCE

(a) Total Gross Payment (sum of Col. G all pages) . . . . _197.59_

(b) Contribution . . . . . . _12.5%_ _24.70_

(c) Adjustments (explain in detail in separate statement . . . .

(d) Total remittance (item b plus or minus item c) . . . . _24.70_

Title of Program _ESPN2 Radio_
Producer _Lee Hunt_

Commercial ☐   Segmented ☐   Participating ☐
Co-op ☐   Sustaining ☐   Audition ☐   Live Repeat ☐
Net ___ Regional ___ Local Station ___
Multiple Stations ___ Foreign only ___
Date(s) of Original Broadcast _9.30_

Time of Broadcast ⇒ from ___ a.m. p.m. to ___ a.m. p.m.

Pre-recording ☐   Broadcast (24 hrs) ☐
Re-play (use #) ___ Syndication (use #) ___
Foreign area ⇒ use # ___ area # ___
Recording Date(s) ___
Date(s) Recording Used ___
Commercial Announcement ☐   Dramatized Comm'l ☐
Cut-in ☐   Hitch-hike ☐   Cow-catcher ☐
Dramatic Signature ☐   Signature Number ☐
If payment is in 15-min. units, specify number of units ___
If payment is for segments, specify number of segments ___

(A) Social Security Account Number	(B) PERFORMER'S NAME Last	First	Middle Initial	(C) Category	Rehearsal (D) Date	(E) hours From	To	(F) Specify Broadcast Date(s) for each performer	(G) Gross Payment
	CA Thomas Sandy (Santos Castellano)								179.63
								10%	17.96

4/91

Be sure to check instruction sheets and key chart to avoid errors.

TO HEALTH & RETIREMENT OFFICE WITH CHECK

This contract was for a TV session.

ELEVISION PROGRAMS and **AFTRA** H&R REMITTANCE REPORT;PRODUCTION REPORT

IMPORTANT ⇒ Make checks payable to AFTRA HEALTH AND RETIREMENT FUNDS and mail this report to the H&R office in New York, Chicago, or Los Angeles (address below) depending on city in which TV programs covered by this report are made. If city other than New York, Chicago or Los Angeles, contact the local AFTRA office for information. Use this form for live or recorded programs, including repeats or re-plays, and live commercials.

260 MADISON AVENUE, NEW YORK 10016   307 N. MICHIGAN AVE., CHICAGO 60601   6922 HOLLYWOOD BLVD., HOLLYWOOD 90028

HEALTH and RETIREMENT

Reporting Co. _Lee Hunt Assoc_
73 Springst #403
Address _N.Y._

Account No. _38012_ Date _9·30·93_

Signature _Jennn. Taylu_

·is sheet is page _1_ of _1_ pages.
(Use additional sheets if more space needed)

HEALTH AND RETIREMENT REMITTANCE

(a) Total Gross Payment (sum of Col. H all pages) . . . . _737_

(b) Contribution . . . . _10.5%_   _77.39_

(c) Adjustments (explain in detail in separate statement) . . . . _____

(d) Total remittance (item b plus or minus item c) . . . . _77.39_

Title of Program _ESPN 2_
Producer _Lee Hunt_
Commercial ☐ Sustaining ☐ Audition ☐
Net _____ Regional _____ Local Station _____
Multiple Stations _____ Foreign only _____
Date(s) of Original Broadcast ____ ' ___ _9·28_
Time of Broadcast ⇒ from ____ a.m. ____ to ____ a.m.
                              p.m.   p.m.
Pre-recording ☐ Live Broadcast ☐ Repeat ☐ Simulcast ☐
On Air Promo ☐   Video Tape ☐   Other ☐
Re-play (use #) _____ Syndication (use #) _____
Foreign area → use # _____ area # _____
Recording Date(s) _____
Date(s) Recording Used _____

Use this box for reporting one or more of the following when not reported as part of above program.
Live Announcements ☐   Opening, Closing, Etc. ☐
Hitch-hike ☐   Cow-catcher ☐   Cut-in ☐   News insert ☐
News Service ☐   Pooled News or Public Special Event ☐

(A)	(B)				(C)		Rehearsal Schedule and Total Hours Rehearsed				(H)		(I)
Social Security Account Number	PERFORMER'S NAME			Category	Dates		From (E) Time Specified in original call	Tu	From (F) To Actual Time of Rehearsal	Hours (G)	Straight Time	Time & Half	Other Fees	Gross Payment
	Last	First	Middle Initial	(D)									
	Thomas Sanoy												670
	6 promo tags												
	205. 1st					= 205							
	93 eachadd'l.					= 465							
						670					10%		67

In Col (i) enter total gross payment due the performer, including any commission, whether or not the commission is deducted from the overscale payment made. Enter commission Col (H), if known.

4/91   **TO HEALTH & RETIREMENT OFFICE WITH CHECK**

A SAG contract from a national commercial Sandy voiced for Pontiac.
This ran on network TV—a home run in the voice-over industry.

| | **EXHIBIT A** | PERFORMER'S COPY |

STANDARD SCREEN ACTORS GUILD EMPLOYMENT CONTRACT FOR TELEVISION COMMERCIALS

Date ___Aug 2___ , 19 93

Between ___D'Arcy, Masius, Benton & Bowles___ , Producer, and

___Sandy BBM Thomas SANDY CASTELLANO___ Performer. Producer engages
Performer and Performer agrees to perform services for Producer in television commercials as follows:

Commercial Title(s) and Code No(s) _____ No. of Commercials ___(1)___

GMPH0044 "Late Call"

Check if Applicable
☐ Dealer Commercial(s)
  ☐ Type A
  ☐ Type B
☐ Seasonal Commercial(s)
☐ Test or Test Market Commercial(s)
☐ Non-Air Commercial(s)
☐ Produced for Cable

Such commercial(s) are to be produced by ___DMB&B___ , ___Bloomfield Hills, MI___ ,
                                        Advertising Agency   Address
acting as agent for ___Pontiac Motor Division___   ___Bonneville___
                        Advertiser   Product(s)
City and State in which services rendered: ___NY, NY___   Place of Engagement: ___I.P.M. FULLHOUSE___ PRODUCTION

(X) Principal Performer   ( ) Solo or duo   ( ) Signature - solo or duo
( ) Stunt Performer   ( ) Group-3-5   ( ) Group-Signature-3-5
( ) Specialty Act   ( ) Group-6-8   ( ) Group-Signature-6-8
( ) Dancer   ( ) Group-9 or more   ( ) Group-Signature-9 or more
( ) Singer   ( ) Contractor   ( ) Pilot

Classification: On Camera _____ Off Camera ___XX___ Part to be Played ___V/O Anncr.___

Compensation: ___Union scale___ Date & Hr. of Engagement: ___AUG. 2, 1993___ 9:30

Check if: Flight Insurance ($10) Payable ☐
        Wardrobe to be furnished by Producer ☐ by Performer ☐

    If furnished by Performer, No. of Costumes @ $15.00 @ $25.00   Total Wardrobe Fee $
                                            (Non-Evening Wear) (Evening Wear)
    ☐ Performer does not consent to the use of his/her services in commercials, made hereunder as dealer commercials payable at dealer
      commercial rates.
    ☐ Performer does not consent to the use of his/her services in commercials made hereunder on a simulcast.

The standard provisions printed on the reverse side hereof are a part of this contract. If this contract provides for compensation at SAG minimum,
no addition, changes or alterations may be made in this form other than those which are more favorable to the Performer than herein provided. If
this contract provides for compensation above SAG minimum, additions may be agreed to between Producer and Performer which do not conflict
with the provisions of the SAG Commercials Contract, provided that such additional provisions are separately set forth under "Special Provisions"
hereof and signed by the Performer.

Until Performer shall otherwise direct in writing, Performer authorizes Producer to make all payments to which Performer may be entitled hereunder
as follows:

    ☐ To Performer at ___235 INGHAM, ELLOTT, DIDINE (NEW YORK___
                                            (Address)

    ☐ To Performer c/o _____ at _____
                                            (Address)

All notices to Performer shall be sent to the address designated above for payments and, if Performer desires, to one other address as follows:

    To _____
            (Name)   (Address)

All notices to Producer shall be addressed as follows:
    To Producer at ___D'Arcy, Masius, Benton & Bowles, 1725 N. Woodward, Box 811, Bloomfield Hills,___
                                            (Address)   MI 48303

This contract is subject to all of the terms and conditions of the applicable Commercials Contract. Employer of Record for income tax and unemployment insurance purposes is ___Talent Partners___

PRODUCER (NAME OF COMPANY) _____

BY _____   PERFORMER ___Sandy Carl___

Performer hereby certifies that he/she is 21 years of age or over. (If under 21 years of age this contract must be signed below by a parent or guardian.)

I, the undersigned hereby state that I am the _____ of the above named Performer and do hereby consent and give my permission to this agreement.   (Mother, Father, Guardian)

                                            _____
                                            (Signature of Parent or Guardian)

SPECIAL PROVISIONS (including adjustments, if any, for Stunt Performers):

Performer acknowledges that he/she has read all the terms and conditions in the Special Provisions section above and hereby agrees thereto.

                                            _____
                                            (Performer)

            IMPORTANT PROVISIONS ON BACK. PLEASE READ CAREFULLY.

(W-4 FORM IS ATTACHED HERE)

Back of the SAG contract from the previous page lists standard provisions of the contract.

STANDARD PROVISIONS

1. **RIGHT TO CONTRACT**

    Performer states that to the best of his/her knowledge, he/she has not authorized the use of his/her name, likeness or identifiable voice in any commercial advertising any competitive product or service during the term of permissible use of commericial(s) hereunder and that he/she is free to enter into this contract and to grant the rights and uses herein set forth.

2. **EXCLUSIVITY**

    Performer states that since accepting employment in the commercial(s) covered by this contract, he/she has not accepted employment in nor authorized the use of his/her name or likeness or identifiable voice in any commercial(s) advertising any compeitive product or service and that he/she will not hereafter, during the term of permissible use of the commercial(s) for which he/she is employed hereunder, accept employment in or authorize the use of his/her name or likeness or identifiable voice in any commercial(s) advertising any competitive product or service. Unless otherwise bargained for, this paragraph shall not apply to off-camera solo or duo singers or group performers other than name groups or to performers employed in Seasonal Commercials under Section 39 of the SAG Commercials Contract.

3. **OTHER USES (Strike "a" or "b" or both if such rights not granted by Performer)**

    (a)   Foreign Use

    Producer shall have the right to the foreign use of the commercial(s) produced hereunder, for which Producer agrees to pay performer not less than the additional compensation provided for in the SAG Commercials Contract. Producer agrees to notify SAG in writing promptly of any such foreign use.

    (b)   Theatrical & Industrial Use

    Producer shall have the right to the commercial(s) produced hereunder for theatrical and industrial use as defined and for the period permitted in the SAG Commercials Contract, for which Producer shall pay performer not less than the additional compensation therein provided.

4. **ARBITRATION**

    All disputes and controversies of every kind and nature arising out of or in connection with this contract shall be subject to arbitration as provided in Section 56 of the SAG Commercials Contract.

5. **PRODUCER'S RIGHTS**

    Performer acknowledges that performer has no right, title or interest of any kind or nature whatsoever in or to the commercial(s). A role owned or created by Producer belongs to Producer and not to the performer.

CEC 9-88

Double scale national network is a huge score for a voice talent. Sandy did 6 commercials in a campaign for Stouffer Hotels through Wyse Advertising. This is one of the SAG contracts from that campaign.

MAR-26-1993 14:28 FROM WYSE ADVERTISING, INC   TO   13056549090   P.04

EXHIBIT "A"

STANDARD AFTRA EMPLOYMENT CONTRACT FOR RADIO COMMERCIALS (Excluding Extras)

SANTO CASTELLANO

Date __3/26__, 19 __93__

Between __Wyse Advertising__ Producer, and __Sandy Thomas__, Performer.
Producer engages Performer and Performer agrees to perform services for Producer in television commercials as follows:

Date of Engagement __March 26, 1993__

Time & Place of Engagement __3:30 p.m. - Love 94__

For __Wyse Adv.__ and __Stouffer Hotels & Resorts__
(Advertising Agency)   (Advertiser)

Address __24 Public Square, Cleveland, OH 44113__

Product __Hotels__   No. of Commercials __1__

Check if Applicable:
☐ Dealer Commercial(s)
☐ Type A
☐ Type B
☐ Seasonal Commercial(s)
☐ Test Market Commercial(s)
☐ "Non Air" Commercial(s)

Employer of record for income tax and unemployment

Commercial ID __SFHR-267-60__   Insurance purposes is __Wyse Advertising__
☐ Performer does not consent to the use of performer's services in commercials made hereunder as dealer commercials payable at dealer commercial rates.
☐ Performer does not consent to the use of performer's services in commercials made hereunder on a simulcast.

CLASSIFICATION:
()Actor
XX Announcer (Commercial)
()Announcer (Program)
()Closing, Standard lead-ins & Hand-outs
()Stunt Performer
()Puppeteer
()Specialty Act

()On Camera   ()Off Camera
()Singer or Dancer solo or duo
()Group 3-5
()Group 6-8
()Group 9 or more
()Contractor

XX Radio
()Singer-Signature-solo or duo
()Group-Signature-3-5
()Group-Signature 6-8
()Group-Signature - 9 or more
()Pilot

Session Fee
(On-Camera Performers)

Session Fee
Radio
__Double Scale__

Compensation:
Check if: Flight Insurance ($10) Payable ☐
Wardrobe to be furnished by Producer ☐ by Performer ☐ $_____
If furnished by Performer, No. of Garments
Non-Evening Wear ___
Evening Wear ___   Total Wardrobe Fee $_____

The standard provisions printed on the revenue side hereof are a part of this contract. If this contract provides for compensation at minimum AFTRA scale, no addition, changes or alterations may be made in this form either than those which are more favorable to the performer than herein provided.

If this contract provides for compensation above minimum AFTRA scale, additions may be agreed to between Producer and performer which do not conflict with the provisions of the AFTRA TV Recorded Commercials Contract, provided that such additional provisions are separately set forth under "Special Provisions" hereof and signed by the performer.

Performer authorizes Producer to make all payments to which Performer may be entitled hereunder by check payable to Performer and sent to the AFTRA office nearest the city in which the commercial was made.

This contract is subject to all of the terms and conditions of the AFTRA TV Recorded Commercials Contract.
Producer __Wyse Advertising__   Performer __Sandy Castellano__
By __Kristen Armani__
Performer hereby certifies that Performer is 18 years of age or over. (If under 18 years of age this contract must be signed below by a parent or guardian.)

I, the undersigned, hereby state that I am the _____ of the above
(Parent or Guardian)
named Performer and do hereby consent and give my permission to this agreement.

_____
(Signature of Parent or Guardian)

Special Provisions:

Performer acknowledges that Performer has read all the terms and conditions in the Special Provisions section above and hereby agrees thereto.

Performer _____ Social Security Number _____ ___ _____
(W-4 form is attached here)
NOTICE TO PERFORMER: IMPORTANT PROVISIONS ON BACK OF CONTRACT. PLEASE READ CAREFULLY.

These websites and other publications will give you access to people and companies that hire or represent voice talent. It also will provide you with information on credible higher level schools in Journalism and Mass Communications.

www.allaccess.com

www.amazon.com Where it says go...type in the words voice overs. A list of books on voice-overs will appear.

www.backstage.com

www.radioready.com

www.RadioVo.com

www.rapmag.com

www.rronline.com

www.tvistudios.com

www.voiceover.com

www.voiceovernet.com

www.yahoo.com Where it says search...type in the words voice overs.

JOURNALISM AND MASS COMMUNICATION DIRECTORY (ISSN 0895-6545) Is published annually by the Association for Education in Journalism and Mass Communication at the University of South Carolina, Columbia, SC 29208-0251; (803) 798-0271, FAX: (803) 772-3509. List of major Broadcasting and Journalism colleges.

RADIO AND RECORDS: The *Wall Street Journal* of radio. (310) 788-1625. Order it to find contact names in the radio industry.

NEW YORK SPEECH AND VOICE IMPROVEMENT: 1 (800) SPEAK-WELL.

THE ROSS REPORT: Has lists of Casting Directors, Agents, Production Companies, Ad Agencies and others. Call 1-800-817-3273 for information on how to get this who-to-contact guide. This guide will provide you with major market contacts. The agent list alone is your way to channel your material or voice-over tapes to credible agents that can take your voice-over career to the next level. It is how I got my break.

SAG & AFTRA OFFICES

Arizona/SAG & AFTRA .... (800) 308-2712 or (602) 265-2712

Boston/SAG & AFTRA .... (617) 742-2688

Chicago/SAG & AFTRA .... (312) 573-8081

Cincinnati-Columbus-Dayton-Louisville-Indianapolis
/AFTRA (Tri-State) .... (513) 579-8668

Cleveland .... SAG (216) 579-9305 / AFTRA (216) 781-2255

Dallas-Ft. Worth/SAG & AFTRA .... (214) 363-8300

Denver-Nevada-New Mexico-Utah
/SAG & AFTRA .... (800) 559-7517 or (303) 757-6226

Detroit/SAG & AFTRA .... (248) 355-3105

Florida .... SAG (305) 670-7677 / AFTRA (305) 652-4824

Central Florida .... SAG (407) 649-3100 / AFTRA (407) 354-2230

Georgia/SAG & AFTRA .... (404) 239-0131

Hawaii/SAG & AFTRA .... (808) 596-0388

Houston/SAG & AFTRA .... (713) 972-1806

Kansas City/AFTRA .... (816) 753-4557

Los Angeles .... SAG (213) 954-1600 / AFTRA (213) 634-8100

Minneapolis-St. Paul/SAG & AFTRA .... (612) 371-9120

Nashville/SAG & AFTRA .... (615) 327-2944

Nevada/SAG .... (702) 737-8818

New Orleans/AFTRA .... (504) 822-6568

New York .... SAG (212) 944-1030 / AFTRA (212) 532-0800

North Carolina/SAG .... (910) 762-1889

Philadelphia/SAG & AFTRA .... (215) 732-0507

Pittsburgh/AFTRA .... (412) 281-6767

Portland/SAG & AFTRA .... (503) 279-9600

Puerto Rico/SAG & AFTRA .... (787) 289-7832

St. Louis/SAG & AFTRA .... (314) 231-8410

San Diego/SAG & AFTRA .... (619) 278-7695

San Francisco/SAG & AFTRA .... (415) 391-7510

Seattle .... SAG (206) 270-0493 / AFTRA (206) 282-7043

Washington-Baltimore/SAG & AFTRA .... (301) 657-2560

AFTRA Locals and Chapters

ATLANTA (404) 239-0131, fax (404) 239-0137
Ms. Melissa Goodman, Executive Director
455 E Paces Ferry Rd NE Ste 334, Atlanta GA 30305

BOSTON (617) 742-2688, fax (617) 742-4904
Ms. Donna Sommers, Executive Director
11 Beacon St # 512, Boston MA 02108

BUFFALO (716) 879-4985
Mr. Rick Pfeiffer, President
c/o WIVB-TV, 2077 Elmwood Ave, Buffalo NY 14207

CHICAGO (312) 573-8081, fax (312) 573-0318
Ms. Eileen Willenborg, Executive Director
1 E Erie Ste 650, Chicago IL 60611

Milwaukee Office (414) 291-9041, fax (414) 291 9043
Mr. Todd Ganser, Bus. Rep.
301 N Water St Flr 4, Milwaukee WI 53202

CLEVELAND (216) 781-2255, fax (216) 781-2257
Mr. Stephen Hatch, Executive Director
1030 Euclid Ave Ste 429, Cleveland OH 44115-1504

DALLAS/FT. WORTH (214) 363-8300, fax (214) 363-5386
Mr. Ken Freehill, Executive Director
6060 N Central Expressway # 302, L.B. 604, Dallas, TX 75206

DENVER (303) 757-6226, fax (303) 757-1769
Mr. Jerry Hookey, Executive Director
950 S Cherry St # 502, Denver CO 80246

DETROIT (248) 355-3105, fax (248) 355-2879
Ms. Barbara Honner, Executive Director
27770 Franklin Rd, Southfield MI 48034

FRESNO (209) 252-1655

Mr. Peter Cleaveland

4831 E Shields Ave Ste 32, Fresno CA 93726

HAWAII (808) 596-0388, fax (808) 593-2636

Ms. Brenda Ching, Executive Director

949 Kapiolani Blvd Ste 105, Honolulu HI 96814

HOUSTON (713) 972-1806, fax (713) 780-0261

Mr. Jack Dunlop, Executive Director

2400 Augusta Dr Ste 264, Houston TX 77057

KANSAS CITY (816) 753-4557, fax (816) 753-1234

Mr. Donald Scott, Acting Executive Director

PO Box 32167, 4000 Baltimore Flr 2, Kansas City MO 64111

LOS ANGELES (323) 634-8100, fax (323) 634-8246

Mr. John Russum, Executive Director

5757 Wilshire Blvd, Hollywood CA 90036-3689

MIAMI (305) 652-4824 or (305) 652-4846, fax (305) 652-2885

Ms. Diane Hogan, Executive Director

20401 N W 2nd Ave # 102, Miami FL 33169

Orlando Office

Ms. Lorraine Lawless, Central Florida Rep

(407) 354-2230, fax (407) 354-2219

(Miami) 1-(800) 330-AFTR

Major Building, 5728 Major Blvd Ste 264, Orlando FL 32819

Puerto Rico Office (787) 289-7832 ext. 2312

José Rey, Representative

530 Ponce de Leon Ave Ste 312, Puerto de Tierra, San Juan, PR 00902

MILWAUKEE (see Chicago)

NASHVILLE (615) 327-2944, fax (615) 329-2803
 Mr. Randall Himes, Executive Director
 PO Box 121087, 1108 17th Ave S, Nashville TN 37212

NEW ORLEANS (504) 822-6568, fax same
 Mr. Bob McDowell, Executive Director
 2475 Canal St Ste 108, New Orleans LA 70119

NEW YORK (212) 532-0800, fax (212) 545-1238
 Mr. Stephen Burrow, Executive Director
 260 Madison Ave Flr 7, New York NY 10016

OMAHA (402) 346-8384
 Mr. Bob Horder
 3000 Farnham St Ste 3-East, Omaha NE 68131

ORLANDO (see Miami)

PEORIA (309) 698-3737
 Mr. Garry Moore, Treasurer
 c/o Station WEEK-TV, 2907 Springfield Rd, East Peoria IL 61611

PHILADELPHIA (215) 732-0507, fax (215) 732-0086
 Mr. John Kailin, Executive Director
 230 S Broad St Ste 500, Philadelphia PA 19102

PHOENIX (602) 265-2712, fax (602) 264-7571
 Mr. Donald Livesay, Executive Director
 1616 E Indian School Rd # 330, Phoenix AZ 85016

PITTSBURGH (412) 281-6767, fax (412) 281-2444
 Mr. Mark Wirick, Executive Director
 625 Stanwix St, The Penthouse, Pittsburgh PA 15222

PORTLAND (503) 279-9600, fax (503) 279-9603
 Mr. Stuart Pemble-Belkin, Executive Director
 3030 S W Moody Ste 104, Portland OR 97201

ROCHESTER (716) 467-7982
Ms. June Baller, President
87 Fairlea Dr, Rochester NY 14622

SACRAMENTO/STOCKTON (916) 455-3870
Mr. Michael McLaughlin, President
4530 Attawa Ave, Sacramento CA 95822

SAN DIEGO (619) 278-7695, fax (619) 278-2505
Mr. Thomas W. Doyle, Executive Director
7827 Convoy Ct # 400, San Diego CA 92111

SAN FRANCISCO (415) 391-7510, fax (415) 391-1108
Mr. Frank Du Charme, Executive Director
235 Pine St Flr 11, San Francisco CA 94104

SCHENECTADY/ALBANY (518) 374-5915
Mr. Jim Leonard, President
170 Ray Ave, Schenectady NY 12304

Mr. Peter Rief, Shop Coordinator (518) 452-4800
c/o WGY-AM/WRVE-FM, 1 Washington Square, Albany NY 12205

Mr. Jack Aernecke & Mr. Peter Brancato, Shop Coordinators
(518) 346-6666
c/o WRGB-TV, 1400 Balltown Rd, Schenectady NY 12309

SEATTLE (206) 282-2506, fax (206) 282-7073
Mr. John Sandifer, Executive Director
601 Valley St # 100, Seattle WA 98109

ST. LOUIS (314) 231-8410, fax (314) 231-8412
Ms. Jackie Dietrich, Executive Director
1310 Papin Ste 103, St. Louis MO 63103

TRI-STATE (513) 579-8668, fax (513) 579-1617 (includes Cincinnati, Columbus & Dayton, OH; Indianapolis, IN & Louisville, KY)
Ms. Herta Suarez, Executive Director
128 E 6th St # 802, Cincinnati OH 45202

TWIN CITIES (612) 371-9120, fax (612) 371-9119
Ms. Colleen Aho, Executive Director
708 N 1st St Ste 333-Itasca Bldg, Minneapolis MN 55401

WASHINGTON/BALTIMORE (301) 657-2560, fax (301) 656-3615
Ms. Pat O'Donnell, Executive Director
4340 E West Highway # 204, Bethesda MD 20814

My sister, Lois. She helps run my office.

Glossary

ADI

(Area of Dominant Influence) A standard geographical area, composed of a number of counties where local TV or radio stations dominate.

AFTRA

(American Federation of Television & Radio Artists) A union for announcers. To learn more about AFTRA, contact an AFTRA office listed in this book.

ASCAP

(The American Society of Composers, Artists, and Publishers) A music licensing organization.

Account

An advertiser, a client.

Actuality

A recording or broadcast live at an event.

Ad Lib

An unrehearsed spontaneous vocal message.

Affidavit

A sworn statement certifying that certain commercials or live announcements were broadcast on a certain day.

Affiliate

A radio station or TV station that associates itself with a network and runs some of their programming.

Afternoon Drive

The time frame most workers commute in the afternoon usually between 3 p.m.–7 p.m.

Agent

A person, or group of individuals, that represent you as a voice-over artist and are instrumental in gaining you employment opportunities by way of auditions and castings. Some agents require exclusive agreements, some do not. Most agents will also take on the task of processing your payment by billing the client, subtracting their commission and forwarding the balance to you, after standard tax deductions are made.

Aircheck

A recorded portion of a radio show for demonstration purposes.

Airshift

The scheduled time period of work of an on air personality, usually referring to a radio Disc Jockey.

Announcement

A commercial or non-commercial message. The industry term is usually referred to as "spot"—when you hear it spoken, do not look to your shirt for a stain.

Announcer

An individual performing a voice-over is referred to as an announcer.

Audio

Transmission, reception or reproduction of sound.

Audition

Everything you live for. An audition is your gateway to employment. A trial performance for voice-over talent where you will read voice-over copy, and be required to voice the specific voice-over project. You could be auditioning for a commercial, promo work, animation, or various other types of voice-over work. Auditions take place at various locations, your agent's agency, an advertising agency or casting director studios. Copy might be faxed to you.

Availabilities, or Availables

Specific commercial time slots on a commercial radio or TV station that are open for commercial usage.

BMI

(Broadcast Music Incorporated) A music licensing organization.

Back-time

The process where an audio or sound engineer times an audio/sound segment from the point it ends, rather than from the point it begins.

Background

What is put behind the voice-over. Usually music or sound effects.

Bed

NO, not where you sleep. In voice-over land it refers to the music that lays behind the voice-over.

Billing
The amount a company bills for advertising revenue.

Bird
A communication satellite.

Bit part
A small part in a play or movie.

Block
A segment of log, or programming blocked out, or reserved.

Board
The audio console from which the audio engineer operates. The board is the main center where electronic signals, including your voice, are initially contained. From the board the audio engineer will either mix the various elements, or further route them to another source.

Booking
A commitment that you have been chosen to be the voice on a particular account.

Boom
Overhead mic stand.

Booth
An enclosed, usually sound proofed, room where the voice talent will usually work.

Break up
Usually refers to vocal audio becoming distorted and un-usable. To say "You're breaking up" means your voice is technically distorting. It is usually due to line problems when transferring audio via ISDN, or can be due to equipment problems.

Bump

Refers to allotment of time when booking a voice-over talent.

Call Letters

The letters assigned to a radio station by the FCC.

Cold Read

Copy read with no music accompaniment.

Commercial

An announcement which advertises a product, service or certain institutions. A commercial is also referred to as a spot.

Compression

To compress is to add dynamic range to one's voice. Too much compression can ruin the sound of the human voice, therefore, compression functions should only be performed by skilled engineers.

Console

Same as the board. A large desk like piece of equipment where the audio engineer monitors, records and mixes the voice-over session.

Copy

Same as the script. Copy is what you will read at your voice-over job.

Cue

A signal given, either electronically or physically, to start a particular announcement.

Cut

Refers to a particular voice-over segment.

Dead Air-Time

On TV or radio, when nothing is being broadcast.

Decibel

A unit for measuring the intensity of sound. Zero would be no sound, 130 decibels would cause pain to your ears.

Deejay, or DJ

The person you hear talking on a music formatted radio station, besides on the commercials—an image voice.

Demographics

Statistics used in broadcasting that divide the population in a given market into groups by age, sex, education, income, etc.

Director

Person at a voice-over session responsible for giving you voice direction.

Distortion

An inaccurate reproduction of a signal caused by change in the frequency of the output wave.

Documentary

An extended news program which examines a particular subject, maybe a societal problem, or a subject that is non-problematic.

Donut

A voice-over recorded between a recorded opening and closing, usually that will not be the voice of the DJ or announcer.

Downlink

An earth reviving station.

Drive time

The most frequently listened to times on the radio usually between 6 a.m. to 10 a.m. and 3 p.m. to 7 p.m.

Dub or Dubbing

The transfer of recorded material from one source to another. Perhaps, you will dub from a Beta tape to a VHS tape, or you could dub from a CD to a DAT tape, etc. The final transfer is referred to as the dub. "Here is the dub you requested."

Earphones

A device placed on your ears, used at voice-over sessions when other program elements, maybe music, must be heard by the voice talent, but cannot be picked up by a live microphone. They are also called "Phones," "Cans" or "Headsets."

Echo

A repetition of sound.

Editing

Removal, addition or re-arrangement of taped programmed material. Your voice elements can be spaced apart, words can be removed or shifted. To perform this function is to edit your voice. "Don't worry about that mistake we can edit that out and make it work."

Engineer

The engineer is the person that operates the equipment during your voice-over session.

Equalization

Also called EQ for short. To EQ is to accentuate certain frequencies which will result in an alteration of the sound of your voice. This function is performed by the audio engineer. To EQ requires experience. Do not try it unless you know what your doing.

FCC

(Federal Communications Commission) The federal agency which was created in 1934 to regulate all interstate and foreign communication by wire and radio.

Fade

To increase or decrease the volume of sound.

Feedback

The return of sound which makes a distorted high pitched sound. Usually, not wanted.

Free-lancer

A voice talent not signed exclusively to one agent. Most agents in New York, Los Angeles and Chicago will not accept free-lance arrangements with voice talent. It is usually an exclusive arrangement, or nothing in the major markets.

Gain

The volume of a tone. In your case, the volume of your voice.

Heads

In the old tape format, heads were the mechanical devices used to record, playback or erase information on the tape recorder.

Highs

High frequency sound in the voice. An engineer might say: "Let's lose the high end in the voice."

Hold

When a potential client likes your audition and wants to hold some of your time for a potential booking. A hold is the step before the booking. A client will sometimes try to hold you until the close of business the day before the potential booking. Holds are possibilities. It is better if you do not get your hopes up until your hold turns into a firm booking.

ISDN (Integrated Services Digital Network)

Most people doing voice-overs refer to it as an ISDN line. "Do you have ISDN" means: are you capable of sending your voice via an ISDN line? Besides the ISDN line, which the phone company will install in your studio, you need to purchase something else. The technology needed is a piece of equipment which breaks down your voice digitally and routes it through the ISDN line. This equipment varies. Telos, DRT-128. They all do the same thing, however, some of these ISDN boxes are not compatible with each other. Consult with an audio engineer before your purchase. Chances are that you are buying this equipment because you want to send your voice to your clients, radio stations, TV stations, broadcasting networks and ad agencies. You need to be compatible. That is the key with ISDN transmission. Most up-to-date recording studios have this technology. If you are not working from your own studio, you should ask if ISDN lines are available before you book time.

Insert

A portion of a script where a voice-over might be inserted.

Jingle

Musical commercial.

Level

To get a level is to set your voice projection at the correct point. The engineer and the voice talent will do this before the first take rolls. He might say to you, "Lets get a level." You in return start reading some of the script until he says, "Okay that's good."

Lines

Copy to be read by the voice talent.

Lows

The low frequency of your voice.

Master

The original recording.

Mix

The total compilation of the voice-over; music, if any; sound effects, if any; and other voices if there are multiple voices involved. "How did the final mix sound?"—Means how did the finished product come out?

Modulation

The process of varying the amplitude.

Network

For example: NBC, CBS or ABC. The originator of programs broadcast at the same time on at least two or more affiliated stations.

Off Mike

Not speaking directly into the microphone.

On Mike

To be speaking into the mic. Please tell me you understand this simplistic concept.

Patch

To make an electrical connection for broadcast. To send your voice to Los Angeles from New York via ISDN line is to patch your voice from Los Angeles to New York. Some people refer to it as a phone patch.

Pop

To pop the microphone means your voice sounds are registering too hard into the mic. Certain sounds are sensitive to Popping. The "P" sound is usually the culprit. It usually requires you to take a different angle into the microphone. Popping is not good. As you perform longer you will master the ability to eliminate popping the mic, as they call it. But, do not worry if you do—everyone does it, even the pros.

Pop Filter

A foam like cover for the microphone used in the defense of popping problems.

Producer

The person in charge of the voice-over session. She or he might be directing, or perhaps, the producer brings a director along. It depends on the situation.

Promo

A non-commercial announcement promoting programming.

Punch

When a director or producer says to you, "Give it more punch, they mean read the word or line or section with more intensity.

Punch-in

(Also called pick up) This is the rejoining of a certain piece of copy, or the continuation of the voicing of copy from a certain point. (i.e.; If a line has to be re-voiced, or you could not read all the way through the copy, the engineer has the ability to let you listen back to what you have already recorded, and then at the exact point in the copy, punch-in the record button and have you either re-record or continue recording. This is called the pickup point. The engineer punched in your new voice. To punch in saves time and preserves your voice.

Rating

The measure of who is listening or watching. "What are the ratings of MSNBC?" Means how many people are watching? Ratings are broken down in many categories; by age, sex or time frame, for example.

Read

The style of reading you present as a voice talent.

Release or released

Being dropped from consideration for a particular voice-over job.

Rough Mix

Is the step before the final mix. The engineer plays back the spot to you and says, "Here it is, but keep in mind, this is a rough mix." He is saying, "I haven't completed the final mix."

SAG

(Screen Actors' Guild). A union for actors and performers. To learn more about SAG, contact a SAG office listed in this book.

Scale

A wage that a union voice talent receives. To be scale talent means working for the minimum SAG or AFTRA wages allowed by those unions. Double scale would be the minimum wage times two; Triple scale would be the minimum wage times three, etc.

Take

The recording of one specific piece of voice-over copy. It is called a take.

Talent

A broadcast performer or entertainer. A voice-over artist is also called talent.

Tape

The medium to which a voice-over is recorded.

Tease

The introductory line used to provoke interest.

Tight

Your time frame to read the voice-over copy is tight. To not have a lot of time to read.

Tone

A specific sound.

Track

An industry term that means record. "We are ready to track," means we are ready to record your voice.

Trailer

A commercial produced with the purpose of promoting a motion picture or video release.

VU Meter

A meter which indicates volume units of sound passing through the audio board.

Watt

A unit of electrical power.

I love photography. I took this picture at a golf course in New Jersey. That hole drops 600 feet. My ball landed in the water to the left of the green.